"It's easy to get stuck in a routine of going through the motions of what we feel we should do each day. We need a catalyst to help us break through those barriers. This great book by Julie Cohen is your catalyst. You'll discover how to authentically design your life and work, and live each day with meaning, purpose, and fulfillment."

Mike Robbins
Author, *Be Yourself, Everyone Else Is Already Taken*

"*Your Work, Your Life ... Your Way* is a must read for anyone looking to design and achieve a better work–life balance on their own terms. The book will open your eyes and give you new clarity to what is important and how to be more effective, integral and successful at both work and home."

Deborah Epstein Henry, Esq.
Founder & President
Flex-Time Lawyers LLC

Advance Praise for *Your Work, Your Life ... Your Way: 7 Keys to Work–Life Balance*

"Julie Cohen has provided an easily-digestible manual for tackling the ever-thorny issue about managing the quality of our work and personal lives. There's lots of rich good common sense here, framed to help anyone achieve positive benefits with a practical and tactical approach. Her concept of 'tighten up, then lighten up' is itself worth the price of admission!"

David Allen
Best-selling author of *Getting Things Done: the Art of Stress-Free Productivity* and *Making It All Work: Winning at the Game of Work and the Business of Life*

"Julie Cohen breaks through the unrealistic standards we all hold ourselves to, especially when it comes to the work–life balance challenge. This book is like having a personal friend and coach, right in the comfort of your own home. The kind who gives you life-changing, invaluable and pragmatic advice, making all the difference in the world."

Dr. Robi Ludwig
Psychotherapist, TV Commentator and Author

"Julie Cohen's book, *Your Work, Your Life ... Your Way*, offers a thoughtful, inspiring and practical approach to work–life balance. Her step-by-step approach took away all feelings of overwhelm; while reading it, I thought, 'I can do this!' And in the process I felt like I was sitting down with Julie for a chat about life, work and the meaning of it all. Best of all, I know I'm not alone: the stories she shares show that many of us have the same concerns and are looking for similar solutions to the problem of our busy lives. Divided into logical sections like 'Develop Priorities' and 'Create Boundaries,' I could dip in and out of chapters that resonated with me, reading Julie's sage advice and exploring my own thoughts and feelings on how these issues impact me and my life."

Karyn Greenstreet
Small Business Coach, Passion For Business, LLC

"Have you ever thought to yourself, 'I wish I had time to ...?' If so (and we all have!), read *Your Work, Your Life ... Your Way*. Instead of wishing for these things, you'll enjoy *doing* them—with confidence, balance, and satisfaction."

Larina Kase
Author of *The Confident Leader: How the Most Successful People Go from Effective to Exceptional* and coauthor of *The New York Times* bestseller *The Confident Speaker*

Your Work, Your Life ... Your Way

7 Keys to Work–Life Balance

Julie Cohen
Professional Certified Coach

Library of Congress Control Number: 2009910552
ISBN: 978-0-9842474-0-0

Printed in the United States of America
First Edition

To Nigel and Aaron—
the life in my work–life

Table of Contents

Acknowledgments

I am so fortunate to be surrounded by wonderful people who have supported, encouraged, guided, challenged and motivated me throughout the process of writing this book. Thank you to:

- Karyn Greenstreet for giving me tools to take this initial idea and make it into something useful for my clients.
- Lisa Kramer and Colleen Bracken—two of the best coaches in the world, and dear friends and colleagues, for reminding me of Key 7 almost daily.
- Suzanne Murray of StyleMatters—editor extraordinaire, for crafting my words and ideas miraculously.
- 7 Barriers class participants—for helping me shape the content of this book.
- My clients, past and present—you make me a better coach and person with each interaction.
- My friends/readers/advisors—Janine, Bill, Rachel, Val. Your time and input means so much to me.
- My wise Facebook friends—for being there ready to respond to my queries with insight, wisdom and creativity.
- Melissa Cohen—for unlimited creative and sisterly support.
- Mom and Dad—supporting me and taking care of some of the "life" stuff when "work" took over.
- Nigel and Aaron—for loving me throughout the roller coaster ride. I love you.
- And although too many to mention—friends, neighbors, colleagues and coaches in my community who have given me feedback and provided inspiration to me on my journey.

deliberate choices about how much you work (and why) and as long as you are comfortable with these choices. Instead, this book will help you identify your own preferred mix of work and life, which may involve more work at certain times in your life than at other times.

That being said, you may have come to this book with some interest in bringing more nonwork activities into your life or simply reducing the amount of time and energy you spend at work or even just diminishing the degree of stress your work causes you. As a result, this book will support you in identifying and addressing the actions you take around your professional commitments that infringe on all the other things that are important to you.

Why Am I Writing This Book?

I am writing this book to share the knowledge I have gained from helping individuals identify how their work does not work for them, which often impacts these individuals' overall satisfaction with the balance in their lives between professional and nonprofessional activities.

In my work with clients, I have seen the same work–life balance themes arise time after time, which has ultimately led me to identify 7 common barriers to work–life balance and 7 "keys" that can be used to navigate past these barriers. I have identified these 7 barriers—and 7 keys to navigating them—over years of working with high-achieving professionals who work a lot and want a change.

It is these 7 barriers and keys that are explored in this book. In addition, this book will feature some of the very

Introduction

How often have you said, "My work is killing me!" or "If I only had time, I'd …?" How often have your work responsibilities pulled you away or prevented you from engaging in a more personally, emotionally, spiritually, socially, or [you-fill-in-the-blank] rewarding experience? For most people, the time spent on the work side of the equation is much greater than the time spent enjoying other meaningful endeavors. This is often the catalyst for much stress, discomfort, and maybe even outright anger.

As a career and personal coach, I have worked with hundreds of clients, supporting them in designing more satisfying professional and personal lives. One of the major concerns with almost all of my clients, regardless of what has brought them to work with me, is the desire to create a more balanced mixture of the time they spend working and the time they spend not working. If you feel like many of my clients do—overwhelmed or bothered by a less-than-desirable mix of work and life, you are not alone.

At times, we all make sacrifices in order to uphold our work commitments or to advance professionally. In fact, as you will discover, this book does not treat working a little extra as a situation that is inherently problematic—as long as you are making

List of Fieldwork Exercises

same "fieldwork" I provide to my clients everyday—concrete exercises and activities to support you in creating new ways of operating as an effective professional and a satisfied hobbyist, volunteer, parent, soccer coach, activist, artist … this list goes on and on and will be personalized by you—in sum, to improve your work–life balance and live your life *on your own terms.*

My hope as you read this book and invest time in doing the fieldwork exercises is that you will develop a new perspective that empowers you to call the shots in your work and life choices. No longer will you be driven by external forces that do not have your best interests in mind. No longer will you assume that there is only one way to work. No longer will you feel the struggle of never having enough … time, energy, sleep, or choices. Again, you get to "fill in the blank."

As you notice, you get to "fill in the blank" a lot. It is really up to you on how to design your work and your life—so that they work for you—and my intentions in this book are to guide you in that process. I believe that too many of us feel like we do not have control over our own lives, and I am writing this book to help liberate readers from the idea that they have to live their lives on someone else's terms.

Why Read This Book?

You might also be wondering why you should read this particular book when there are several others on the topic of work–life balance floating around the market. So let's look at what this book has to offer and why it might be special and worth your time.

1. *This book uses a hands-on approach that leads to real change.* Reading this book will not only help you to shift your *thinking* about work–life balance, but it will also help shift your way of *acting and interacting* (i.e., your way of behaving). In particular, the many practical exercises included in the book will aid you in translating new thoughts about work–life balance into action. In other words, this book will help you see real results!

2. *This book offers a baby-step approach that makes change doable, not overwhelming.* This book includes all the fundamental steps and exercises I use with clients to help them improve their work–life balance. As you will discover, each chapter is broken down into a series of small, straightforward steps (or exercises) that you can engage in at your own pace to improve your work–life balance bit by bit, over time. This book thus aims to make the change process both manageable and achievable.

3. *The guidance provided in this book is very concrete, solution-oriented, and future-directed so you don't just think about issues, you actually work through them.* Unlike therapeutic approaches, which often have you reflecting on your past to gain a philosophical understanding of why you are the way you are, this book (true to the coaching model) has you focusing on the present and the future. The book's approach also keeps things concrete, encouraging you to identify clear problems that can be solved along with accompanying solutions that are palatable—maybe even exciting—to you. Again, this will help you make tangible changes to your work–life mix.

4. *This book allows you to customize work–life balance to meet your personal priorities and values (not someone else's).* This book encourages you to let go of outside pressure to give attention to some areas of your life more than others and, instead, to design a life that is reflective of what matters most to you.

5. *This book gives you permission to be unbalanced sometimes!* The last thing you need is pressure to be balanced, on top of all the other pressures you likely face day-to-day. This book puts forth a flexible approach that acknowledges that finding balance is an ongoing journey that sometimes involves taking purposeful detours, pit stops, and breaks along the way.

Through a customized, flexible, and hands-on approach that is built on baby steps and aimed at using a solution-oriented approach, this book serves as a sort of "coach-in-a-box"—practical, comprehensive support for overcoming your barriers to work–life balance and for putting significant keys to work–life balance into practice. Although you can benefit from supplementing your efforts by enlisting the help of a real, live person— such as a coach, a mentor, or a friend on a similar journey—this book will nonetheless provide you with a useful guide to making lasting and satisfying changes to your work–life balance.

Work–Life Balance Defined

Since this book focuses on the concept of work–life balance, I would like to define what I mean by this term. Interestingly, when discussing work–life balance with my clients and asking many groups of people what work–life balance means to them, I always receive a varied range of answers. For some, it is a feeling of peacefulness around how they operate; for others, it is the ability to accomplish all that they want. For me, it is having the flexibility to make work and life choices that are best for my current situation without worry. For my husband, it is having enough time at home with our son while enjoying his work, hobbies, and friends. When I ask an audience at a presentation this question, I get unique answers from each person. Try it yourself—ask a group of friends—what is work–life balance? My hunch is that you will get a great variety of answers.

For the purposes of this book, I will be using the following definition to represent what I mean by *work–life balance*. When I mention the term in this book, I am referring to your more desired approach to integrating your work and non-work commitments, responsibilities, and activities. The term is also meant to describe an ideal state or situation in which your personal priorities have the space and energy needed to be addressed while also allowing for work requirements, accomplishments, and desires.

On the Term *Work–Life Balance*

When I started creating this material for the book, *work–life balance* was the widely used and accepted terminology. Recently, however, the term's use has been questioned.

As I will discuss later in this *Introduction*, balance as a state is very difficult to attain and almost impossible to maintain. Some people writing about this topic are concerned that using the phrase *work–life balance* sets people up for failure by implying that balance can be captured or permanently attained. In response to this concern, a few other terms have been coined to better capture this more desired process or state that leads to greater satisfaction in both personal and professional realms.

As I began the second round of edits for this book, I was greatly concerned as to whether I needed to find a more appropriate and manageable term beside *work–life balance* to use in the book and the book's title. I did a lot of research, spoke with a wide array of professionals who work in fields that regularly address work–life issues, and started discussions with anyone who was willing to talk. I was certain that the term *work–life balance* was unattainable, inappropriate, and passé and that I *must* find or coin a new phrase to define this very real struggle with which so many people grapple regularly.

As a result, I conducted extensive market research to help select from two new terms I had generated with the help of a small focus group: *work–life satisfaction* and *work–life fulfillment*. These terms seemed much more appropriate, attainable, personal, and positive than simply *work–life balance*. I was on my way to a new and much improved term that would empower my readers, students, and clients.

Yet, after distributing a survey to 500 people, excitedly awaiting the survey responses, and then reading through the results, what I was truly hoping for did not actually happen. My hope was that a large percentage of the survey respondents would strongly prefer one of my focus group phrases and it would be an easy and obvious switch to a new title and term throughout the book. Unfortunately, that was not the case. Instead, the preference between the two predefined phrases was almost equal. So, I did not easily have a new title or a new phrase to "brand."

Although I did not get my hoped-for "silver bullet," I did get so much more. Generous survey respondents poured out their thoughts, feelings, and creativity. At least thirty phrases were shared, including *work–life synergy, life optimization, work–life management, work–life alignment, life/work satisfaction, work–life fusion, work–life integration*, and *work–life flow*.

In response to "my" two terms, there were many unique perspectives. People loved and hated each phrase. A group also strongly preferred *work–life balance* as they felt it was "the" term that people understood—the common, most used, and most understood phrase for what I wanted to describe. As one respondent said, "a pig with lipstick is still a pig"—meaning, no matter what I decided to call the book or which phrase to use throughout it, the term *work–life balance* would be most identifiable and understandable by the largest audience.

So, with these wise words, and thirty-three pages of passionate feedback, I have decided to keep the term *work–life balance* in the title and throughout the book.

Since for the purposes of this book I am defining work–life balance generically—as a more desired approach to integrating your work and nonwork commitments, responsibilities, and activities—I would like to offer the following caveat for you to remember each time you read the phrase *work–life balance*. Please think of *work–life balance* as a shorthand way to represent the many unique perspectives that each person has when working and struggling with the often crazy mix of time, commitments, priorities, and responsibilities that make up one's professional and personal life. No matter what definition represents the concept best for you, the end goal of this book is this: that you will be empowered by the tools, insights, and actions included in this book to ultimately make choices that allow your work–life balance to be uniquely, personally, and optimally defined and implemented by you.

The Myths of Work–Life Balance

The phrase *work–life balance* is heard often in the media with magazines, talk shows, and self-help professionals offering solutions on how to "get it." Yet, this approach often does a great disservice to all of us as it falsely assumes that work–life balance is an end state—something that you can accomplish and then maintain forever. With all due respect—you are never going to get there!

Now that I have stated the truth in its bluntest form, I will refine that point a bit. What I mean to say is that while you might achieve moments or even days of balance, balance is not something you are likely to experience on an absolute or permanent basis. Work–life balance is not so much a steady state to be attained, captured, nailed down, or maintained; instead, it is more of a state to be attempted, approached, or approximated. You might even think of it as a dance, with a few steps in one direction and a few steps in another, all circling around your ideal picture of work–life balance.

To understand this concept more fully, let's look at balance in general. Imagine the following three things: a seesaw (or teeter–totter), a tightrope walker, and a spinning top. When you think of these three things, balance may be what you think they have in common—but let's examine them more closely. In actuality, a seesaw never actually *achieves* balance. It is constantly *moving* in response to the energy and pressure each rider applies. A tightrope walker may look balanced, but she never stops, is always adjusting the pole she is carrying and her center of gravity, and is working very hard to appear somewhat stable. One slip, and she falls. Finally, there is the spinning top. Again, it looks balanced, but only when it is moving quickly. As the top slows down, it begins to wobble, then falls over and stops.

These metaphors—a seesaw, a spinning top, and a tightrope walker—point to one of the greatest myths of work–life balance. Although work–life balance is often envisioned as some

end state to be fully achieved and then maintained permanently (the myth!), in fact, work–life balance is a continual
journey that never stops. Like the seesaw and spinning top that
both move with fluidity for a time when the right actions are
applied, you too can experience the satisfying journey of enjoying more balance in your life. Nonetheless, it is helpful to realize that the journey will involve some hard work and continual
tweaking—as is the case for the tightrope walker. Sometimes
you might even fall off the high wire or choose to jump. Yet,
the good news is that you can always begin the process of balancing once again, when you are ready.

*So, the first myth relevant to this book is that work–life bal-
ance is an end state to be achieved.* In reality, work–life balance
is a continual journey in which to be engaged—a process of
balancing, working, tweaking, adjusting, maybe falling down,
climbing up again, and then reengaging.

There is another important work–life balance myth to consider, too. *This second myth is that work–life balance has a single
definition—that it looks and feels the same to each of us.* Balance
does not necessarily mean working only forty hours a week,
leaving the office by 5 p.m. every night, being at your child's
every soccer game, having time to nurture your hobby, and
sleeping eight hours every night. It may mean this, but it is
going to mean something different for everyone reading this
book and for everyone you know.

As I mentioned earlier in this *Introduction*, each of us actually
has our own personal definition of work–life balance. Once we
give ourselves permission to embrace this reality, it can be both
liberating and empowering ... because we become free to make
choices based on what we want for ourselves, not what we feel

pressured to pursue on the basis of other people's opinions or society's preferences.

For some individuals, ideal work–life balance involves spending a good amount of one's time on professional endeavors; for others, ideal work–life balance involves finding a way to focus mostly on endeavors outside of the professional domain, such as raising children. For others, ideal work–life balance involves finding a more equal mix of professional and personal activities, in which both domains are valued and one does not predominate over the other. And, of course, some people do not even think of their ideal work–life balance in terms of how much time they spend in the professional or the personal domain; instead, they describe their ideal balance in terms of the accomplishments that are most important to them, the kind of "down time" they hope to have, or the feelings they want to experience on an everyday basis.

How you define and frame your ideal work–life balance will be entirely up to you.

Yet, it can be easy to fall into the trap of feeling guilty about your own version of work–life balance. On top of struggling to find balance, you might also find yourself thinking critical thoughts of your personal definition of balance! That is not only unfair to yourself, it is also counterproductive to the process. Ideally, you will let go of any self-doubt you have about your own personal version of ideal work–life balance, and you will give yourself permission as you read this book to embrace this personalized version of what seems right to you. The fieldwork throughout the book will also encourage you to do so.

So, the myths of work–life balance are two-fold: that there is *one* right definition of work–life balance in which each of us needs to fit and that work–life balance is a *destination* at which we eventually arrive and stay—a sort of work–life balance nirvana.

In light of these myths, my goal in this book is to enable you to reframe work–life balance in a much more personal and manageable way. I aim to acknowledge the very personal nature of work–life balance as well as to empower you to create a custom work–life mix that works for you. I also attempt to be honest about the fact that the process of approaching balance requires work and is ongoing. This last point is also meant to take some pressure off of you. Sometimes you will not feel balanced, and that is okay!

Work–Life Balance Is a Journey ...

Thus, work–life balance is a journey toward a destination that you will approach or even "visit" from time to time but to which you most likely will not indefinitely remain.

On this journey toward work–life balance, think of your self-knowledge and your intuition as an internal compass that can tell you when you are veering far off the path or when you are getting closer. This book will encourage you to dig out your compass and learn to trust it.

Admittedly, you will constantly have to readjust your route when you hit unplanned roadblocks, potholes, detours, and traffic jams. You will also experience occasional short cuts, enjoy scenic routes, and be aided by bridges. At times, you will be off the beaten path enjoying the view and at other times you will be in an express lane, missing everything you are passing by. The key to managing the journey is not getting too caught up at where you are any one moment. Over time, whether it is an hour, a day, a week, or a year, you can make choices that move you closer to what balance means to you, accepting that at any one time, there may be instances when things are very far from your ideal.

The goal of this book is to help you become aware of the road hazards you will face, point out more effective routes, show you how to use your own work–life balance compass, and invite you to make choices that put you in a faster lane on your journey in your desired direction.

As mentioned earlier in this *Introduction*, I have observed 7 barriers—or consistent challenges—that often get in the way of achieving a more sane, manageable, and even desirable mix of life and work time commitments and choices. Seven of this book's nine chapters will explore these barriers, help you identify whether they are inhibiting your own journey toward work–life balance, and, if so, work to move past or through these barriers. This last piece is where the 7 keys—or tools for navigating beyond the barriers—come into play.

The 7 keys are solution-oriented tools that you can use to go around, over, under, or through the barriers and continue on your journey toward work–life balance.

If you look up the word *key* in the dictionary, you will find several meanings. The most obvious, perhaps, is the definition of a key as a metal tool used to gain entrance to something. This matches one of the ways that the 7 keys in this book function. Once you get ahold of one of these "keys," you are likely to discover that what was once a barrier can become simply a door to be unlocked. Once through it, you can continue on your way toward greater work–life balance.

On the other hand, by *7 keys* I am also referring to keys as "something that gives an ... identification or provides a solution" as in "the key to a riddle" (*Merriam-Webster Online*). Like the answer key that helps you solve a crossword puzzle or a legend that helps you decipher a map, the 7 keys together serve as a sort of code-breaker for the barriers through which you need to navigate to move toward your desired work–life balance. Instead of seeing these barriers as insurmountable obstacles that cannot be overcome, the keys provide you with tools for navigating past the barriers, much like a road map.

Knowing what gets in the way of your desired work–life balance—that is, identifying the barriers—is the first step in changing your work–life balance to a more preferable state. Once you understand the barriers that are in your way, you will be able to craft new paths and choices to move you further along your desired route—using the keys described and the fieldwork exercises presented.

How to Use This Book

As you can see by the description of work–life balance thus far, how balance looks in practice is a very personal choice. What works for you will likely be very different from what works for your best friend, brother or sister, boss, or the stranger next to you on the bus. As work–life balance is personal, so is how you might use this book.

The 7 keys and barriers that follow encompass facets of your life that are personal and professional. They also include situations that impact you externally as well as perspectives that affect you internally. The fieldwork exercises that appear in each chapter are also varied. Some fieldwork requires observation, some requires reflection, and some requires action.

If you are comfortable working in a linear fashion, I recommend that you go through the keys in order, as the book was written. If you come across a key that does not feel relevant to you, skim through the rest of the chapter and start the next. Note that some of the individual pieces of fieldwork may be very useful even if the relevant barrier is not a primary challenge for you. And, as there is some overlap and connection among multiple barriers, if you read each chapter, you may become aware of new relationships and solutions to challenges and roadblocks that you did not think were connected.

If working through the book in order does not feel right to you, focus on the keys that seem most relevant to your own journey toward work–life balance. Even so, within a given chapter, do conduct the fieldwork exercises in the order in which they appear, rather than skipping ahead: The fieldwork exercises are meant to build on each other as well as on the earlier text in the chapter.

If you choose to skip around rather than read the book in a linear fashion, I still encourage you not to skip the chapter entitled *Key 5 – Reprioritize Your Values*. People who are dissatisfied with their current work–life balance often find that some incompatibility exists between or among their values. This chapter will help you gain insight into your values and why they matter in regard to work–life balance. This chapter will also engage you in fieldwork exercises that help you more clearly define your values and therefore what matters most to you. I believe this key's fieldwork is particularly important and very useful to everyone; my clients who have focused on this key tend to agree.

A Guide to Doing the Fieldwork

Throughout this book, you will be asked to complete exercises and answer questions while you are reading the book. I refer to these parts of each chapter as *fieldwork*, and you will notice them in the text by a little graphic that says *Fieldwork*. Each fieldwork exercise requires some activity or observation in the context of your work and your life. To get the most out of this book and the concepts being shared, do the work!! As silly as this sounds, change requires change ... which means not only thinking about something differently but also *doing* something differently than you are doing right now.

The start of making changes to the way you work and the way you live your life is marked with an initial action step: In this case, you are making the commitment to read this book, answer questions, and do the fieldwork thoroughly for each key. Change begins with commitment. Are you ready? If so, here are my recommendations for getting the most out of this book.

Step #1: Establish a Dedicated Place to Do the Work in This Book

As you begin this process, decide on one or two locations where you will work on your fieldwork and think about the choices and changes you will be making. Make it a place where there will be no (or, at least, very few) disruptions or distractions, and a place that feels like it is your own space: maybe a quiet coffee shop, your local library, or a comfortable chair in a less-trafficked room in your home. Also, set aside either a file in your computer or a notebook or journal as a private place to commit the work and any additional thoughts or ideas to paper or computer screen. Alternatively, consider picking up a copy of *7 Keys Workbook and Journal*, a special work space I have created to accompany this book (available online at *www.7KeysToWorkLifeBalance.com*). Throughout the book, as you come upon fieldwork exercises, I will refer you to turn to "*your 7 Keys Workbook and Journal* or other dedicated work space." By *dedicated work space*, I am referring to whatever notebook, journal, or computer file you have selected as your spot for capturing the work in which you engage for this book. You can use your dedicated work space to complete the fieldwork exercises and to record your thoughts, ideas, brainstorms, and visions of the future. It is important to actually write or type the answers to each of the fieldwork exercises so that you can take them from your head and commit them to paper or a saved computer file. There is power in making your ideas and plans concrete.

Step #2: Make the Time

I often hear from new participants in my 7 Barriers/7 Keys programs a frequent and similar concern: "I am already too busy and overwhelmed … how am I going to do anything for this class?" This concern would be reasonable if you were about to add more and more to your plate without removing or reshaping what was already there, but this will not be the case. I want to encourage you and challenge you to fully take the plunge, as most of these activities require only a small amount of time—often only a few additional minutes of thinking, observing, brainstorming, imagining, and creating, all with the intention of designing your work and your life, your way. As you are beginning to dive into this book, look at your calendar and actually schedule time to engage in your journey. The way you choose to schedule this time will be unique to you—maybe an hour a week, fifteen minutes each morning, or a chunk of time Sunday evenings to concentrate on this process and your plans to implement, experiment, and invest in meaningful change.

Step #3: Enlist the Support of Others

There is even more power in these exercises when you share your answers with someone else. This could be a friend, trusted colleague, a professional coach, or others with similar desires to foster greater work–life balance. With whomever you choose to share, be sure the person understands that you want and need support and encouragement for each step of this journey.

In addition to the fieldwork exercises in each chapter, note that if you have a copy of the *7 Keys Workbook and Journal*, you will be able to access a list of reflection questions, entitled *Going Deeper*. These questions will provide you with an opportunity to reflect even further on the guidance offered in the book chapter, how it applies to you, and where you are on your journey to putting that key or guidance into practice. In addition to the actual *Going Deeper* questions, ample space is provided in the workbook/journal for you to write down your answers to these reflection questions.

If you would like to deepen or supplement your learning from this book, you may also want to refer to the *List of Resources for Learning More* provided in the Appendix at the back of this book. This list contains a handful of books and websites you can check out to learn more about putting the guidance from this book into practice.

At the end of each chapter, you will see a section entitled *Postcard from the Road*. This section will highlight the key points of the chapter, in order to simplify the integration of awareness of the key and remediation of the barrier. The intention of these reminders is to provide you with simple statements to keep you focused on making small changes that will eventually lead to significant impact.

Finally, when you begin any new journey, it is helpful to consult a map; and, if you ever should feel lost during your journey, a road map will also help you get your bearings—detecting where you are, confirming your desired destination, and tracing the best route to get there. This metaphor certainly applies to your journey toward improved work–life balance. As a result, this book begins with a brief but significant chapter called *A Road Map for the Journey: How Satisfied Are You?* That chapter—and the fieldwork exercises within it—are an essential part of using this book and getting real results in your efforts toward more preferable work–life balance. In particular, you will have an opportunity in that chapter to assess your *current* satisfaction level with your work–life balance and then to describe your *ideal* work–life balance. In the process, you will be plotting where you are on your journey right now in comparison to where you would like to be heading.

Now that you have a clearer understanding of this book's content, what is meant by work–life balance, and how to use this book for maximum benefit, let's begin your journey toward enhanced work–life balance!

A Road Map for the Journey: How Satisfied Are You?

As mentioned in the *Introduction*, your efforts to cultivate work–life balance will involve a *journey* toward your desired work–life picture. When you begin any journey toward a new place, it always helps to know your starting point so you can map a desired route toward your hoped-for destination. Thus, this short but fundamental chapter of the book will engage you in two hands-on exercises for identifying your current state of work–life balance satisfaction (your starting point) and then identifying your desired state of work–life balance (your hoped-for destination). If you think of yourself as having an internal compass and a direction toward which you would like to turn, this chapter will help you get your bearings.

Are You Satisfied With Your Current Work–Life Balance?

Current State of Your Work–Life Satisfaction

To map your starting point on this journey, you can complete the following fieldwork exercise. Doing so will help you gain clarity regarding your level of satisfaction with your current work–life balance situation. (Note that you will also be revisiting this exercise again at the end of the book—and can check in with it throughout the book—to track whether you are moving in your desired direction.)

Identify Your Current Work–Life Balance Satisfaction: Although you can conduct this exercise directly in this book, you may also prefer to take out your *7 Keys Workbook and Journal* or other dedicated work space (journal, notebook, computer file) and complete this exercise there. For this first exercise, you will determine your "Work—Life Balance Satisfaction Level." To do so, select a number between 1 and 10 that rates how satisfied you are with your work–life balance situation right now, with 10 being completely satisfied with the mix of things in your work and life (and therefore you do not need to be reading this book!) and 1 being complete dissatisfaction—you have *no life* in the mix and do not see any way out.

As you think about your Work—Life Balance Satisfaction Level, some things to consider include how satisfied you are with:

- number of hours you work
- level of stress related to work
- time with family/friends
- your ability to explore your hobbies/interests
- your level of volunteering for your community
- your ability to relax
- your quantity and quality of sleep
- your level of accomplishment
- feeling that you are living your life as you want.

After you have considered these different areas of satisfaction, write down the number that best represents your satisfaction level with your current work-life balance situation.

In addition to this specific number, I would also like you to create a concise descriptor of how you feel about your current work–life balance situation. How satisfied are you? Use three words or less to describe how you feel in this regard. For example, you might write ...

Work–Life Balance Satisfaction Level	Descriptor of How I Feel About My Current Work–Life Balance Situation
3	overwhelmed, wiped-out
4	stressed and tired
7	having some fun
2	need change now
9	loving life

The descriptor needs to be concise so you have a clear definition of your current satisfaction with the situation, but other than that, there is no correct answer to this exercise. I would simply like for you to think about your current work–life situation, in order to numerically quantify your level of satisfaction with this current situation, and then to describe in a few words how you *feel* regarding your current work–life balance situation.

To conduct this exercise, please fill in the following blanks (or turn to your *7 Keys Workbook and Journal* or other dedicated work space and conduct the exercise there).

Today's Date: _____

Your Current Work–Life Balance Satisfaction Level (number between 1 and 10): _____

How do you feel about this level (in three words or less):

_____

Now that you have described how you are currently feeling regarding your current work–life balance situation, you have an opportunity to imagine what is possible. As you begin this journey of change toward life and work on your terms, you need to have a compelling picture of your desired destination on your work–life balance journey. (Note that I do not mean to imply that you will arrive and remain permanently at this destination, given that work–life balance involves continual shifting and rebalancing but instead that this destination represents your *ideal* work–life balance state, the one toward which you would like to strive.)

Desired State of Work–Life Balance

To define your more preferred work–life balance state, picture yourself feeling completely satisfied with how your professional and personal responsibilities integrate. See yourself making choices that allow you to feel good about work and nonwork responsibilities. This is the destination toward which you want to be moving. What does it look like? When you imagine yourself getting closer to it, how do you feel? What is the feeling/state/experience toward which you want your compass pointing? The answer that you come up with will allow you to make choices and take actions that will lead you more effectively on your preferred path.

 Describe Your Preferred Work–Life Balance Situation: Here or in your *7 Keys Workbook and Journal* or other dedicated work space, you are going to describe your preferred work—life balance state—one in which the mix of your work and life priorities feels great to you.

What does it look like? What does it feel like? How is it different from now? Write your comments, thoughts, and reflections.

Now, from your previous thoughts and reflections, create a concise descriptor in three words or less (hyphenated words are acceptable if you need them) so you have a clear and specific direction for your journey.

Here are some examples:

- efficient and calm

- time for me

- accomplished, effective, fun

- downtime without email

- work-free weekends

- re-engaged with hobbies.

Now, commit to the direction toward which you are moving (write your three-word descriptor here):

My compass is pointing toward _____

◆ ◆ ◆

The purpose of the previous two fieldwork exercises was (a) to quantify where you are with your work–life balance satisfaction (current state) and (b) to create a compelling description of the kind of work–life balance you crave (desired state). Whenever you find yourself starting to flag on your work–life balance journey—to feel tired, overwhelmed, or off balance—you can remember this three-word descriptor as a reminder of where you want to be heading. Maybe you even want to think of this three-word descriptor as your personal "theme song"—something that is unique to you and can "play" in your head whenever you start to veer off course and need a reminder of your desired direction.

You have personally selected these three words to represent your ideal work, your ideal life … your way. Use them as guideposts on your travels!

Let the Journey Begin …

Now that you know where you are on your journey toward work–life balance and where you are heading, you are ready to resume your "travels." Fasten your seat belt—here we go!

List of the 7 Barriers and 7 Keys

Barrier	Key
1. Problems With Prioritization	1. Develop Priorities
2. Lack of Boundaries	2. Create Boundaries
3. Inefficient Use of Time, Energy, and Attention	3. Manage Your Day Efficiently
4. Unreasonable Expectations	4. Design Reasonable Expectations
5. Incompatible Values	5. Reprioritize Your Values
6. Unbalanced Organizational Culture	6. Navigate an Unbalanced Organizational Culture
7. Lack of Self-Care	7. Engage in Self-Care

KEY 1

Develop Priorities

Have you ever wished you could add another several hours to your day so you could finally catch up on paperwork or take that class for professional development or fit in time to work out? Or, maybe, just maybe, meet a friend for lunch, or read a book for pleasure? Do you ever feel like you are chasing time and you can never keep up?

In this chapter, you will explore an important key to your preferred work–life balance: developing priorities. In particular, the chapter will focus on helping you learn how to expertly prioritize the roles, responsibilities, activities, and engagements that fill your time so that you spend more minutes and hours in the day focusing on what is most important to you and less time spinning your wheels on things that are either unimportant to you or do not move you closer to your desired work–life balance.

Can you use the guidance in this chapter to turn a twenty-four-hour day into a twenty-seven-hour one? Will the chapter teach you how to "do it all?" Unfortunately, these are promises that no one can make, as appealing as they might sound. What I hope the chapter *will* do is help you to explore, practice, and become well skilled at developing (and maintaining!) your priorities.

As you become more and more adept at prioritizing, you will not actually be adding more minutes and hours to your life, but you will be learning how to use those minutes and hours in a way that leaves you feeling satisfied as you end each day. As the chapter is about to reveal, work–life balance is not about learning how to do it all; instead, it is about learning how to focus on doing what is most important to you.

Developing Awareness of the Key

A Closer Look at the Concept

What is prioritization, anyway? It is not a new concept, of course, but it is a very helpful one so let's review its meaning here. A *priority* is a goal, task, or action that takes precedence—that is of significant importance—compared to other goals, tasks, or actions. A related concept, *prioritization* is the act of setting your priorities—deliberately deciding which goals, tasks, and actions are most significant to you and creating a plan to give those areas the most attention in your day.

Priorities are critical to work–life balance because you really cannot "do it all!" As much as you and I might wish we could, the reality is that we only have twenty-four hours in a day, and ideally seven or more of those are dedicated to sleep. I take the time to make this point not to depress you (!) but because an important aspect of achieving work–life balance is actually about realizing that you *cannot* do it all. Once you come to terms with this reality, you will be freed up to make deliberate choices about how you would actually like to spend your time.

In sum, your time and energy are valuable resources! To move toward your preferred work–life balance, the choices that you make on how to use these valuable resources need to be selected and chosen deliberately, on the basis of what is most important to you, to your work, and to your life.

Identifying the Barrier: Problems With Prioritization

If you are feeling stuck on your journey toward work–life balance, it is possible that the barrier you are facing on your path is *problems with prioritization*. People tend to face this particular barrier to work–life balance when they ...

1. do not know their priorities
2. do not know how to implement their priorities, and/or
3. do not know how to resolve the issues preventing them from addressing their priorities.

Do any of these issues resonate as relevant to your own path? Let's take a glimpse into someone who faces problems with prioritization to see what this barrier looks like in the real world.

Margaret is a director in a busy public relations firm. She supervises a staff of six people and is responsible for many high profile and lucrative clients. Her work ethic includes being very accessible to her clients, which often means responding to their needs very quickly—and at all times of the day (and sometimes at night and on weekends). She also believes in mentoring her staff in order to develop them and grow the business. Again, this requires significant availability and responsiveness at all times of day. Margaret enjoys her work, but she feels like it is encroaching on her personal life. She desires more quality time with her two children and husband and would love to find time for regular exercise and some nonwork enjoyment, but she has not figured out how to make these activities priorities in her life. At the end of most work days, she rarely has enough energy for anything but a late dinner and sleep, and, as a result, she feels dissatisfied with how she has spent the last part of her day.

Margaret often ended each day feeling drained and dissatisfied with her personal life. Why? Because Margaret struggled with the skill of prioritization.

For example, although Margaret wanted to fit exercise in somewhere during the work week, she had not taken the time to set exercise as a priority in her life or to schedule exercise into her day. Similarly, she had not yet practiced the skills of keeping lower priority items from getting in the way of her exercise plans. As a result, other activities in her day always ended up taking precedence over exercise, and Margaret never had the time or energy to get to the gym or go for a walk. The only way that Margaret would ever be able to fit exercise into her day would be if she chose to make exercise a priority.

Now that you have seen an example of someone who has hit the barrier of problems with prioritization, think for a minute about your own life. Have you deliberately selected your work and personal priorities, or do you allow the natural course of your day and the people with whom you interact to dictate your priorities? If you are aware of your priorities, do you manage to maintain them most days or weeks, or are they continually falling by the wayside? Depending on your answers to these questions, you may discover that the skill of prioritization is very useful and relevant to your own journey toward work–life balance.

If you face the barrier of problems with prioritization and are ready to overcome this barrier, you will want to practice the following three behaviors:

1. developing your priorities
2. implementing your priorities
3. resolving the issues stopping you from maintaining your priorities.

These three behaviors are used on a regular basis by people skilled at prioritization.

The next section of the chapter will provide insight into how you can go about practicing these three behaviors to ultimately enhance your desired work–life balance.

Putting the Key Into Practice

As stated previously, people who are good at prioritization typically know what their priorities are, know how to implement their priorities, and know how to resolve the issues stopping them from maintaining their priorities. But let's get even more tactical about how one can go about achieving these three things, so you can roll up your sleeves and start making desired adjustments to your work–life balance.

People good at prioritizing . . .

1. know what their priorities are → because they take the time to develop a personal and professional vision
2. implement their priorities → by using a planning process

3. resolve issues impeding them from maintaining their priorities → by managing low-priority creep.

If you are starting to realize (or be reminded!) that work–life balance could become more manageable for you if you sharpened your prioritization skills, then the rest of the chapter will provide you with practical guidance on how to use this powerful key.

Developing Your Personal and Professional Vision

Let's start with the first of the three points just mentioned— creating a vision. To define your priorities, you need to know what you want to accomplish in your work and in the bigger picture of your life. I call this your *vision*. Without a vision, you may make haphazard choices based on many factors that may not include what is most important to you. With a vision— an image or outline of your most important personal, professional, and work–life balance goals—you can make sound decisions when faced with competing demands on your time, energy, and focus.

In short, a clear vision allows for easier decision-making regarding how you spend your valuable resource of time.

When faced with the task of creating a vision, many people become overwhelmed with what they perceive as the lofty nature of the concept. If that is how you are feeling, then let me give you permission right now that your vision does not have to be lofty at all, just something that feels right and gets you excited. While some people's vision may be to end world poverty or to stop global warming, your personal or professional vision might also be very simple and very local. "Get promoted to director" or "be actively engaged in my daughter's school while running my business" are perfect visions, too. Since this book is about your personal image of your ideal, balanced life, you get to define your vision any way that you want.

As you develop your vision, consider both areas of your life—personal and professional. You may find that one area needs more work or draws your attention more than another, and that is fine, too. I am simply inviting you to create a holistic vision since it is often hard to focus on either the personal or professional area in a vacuum—one almost always affects the other.

Lastly, there is no one correct way to determine your vision. What is critical here is for you to find some method of developing your vision so you have the road map you need to develop and prioritize the goals, tasks, and activities that support that vision. Here are some of the techniques I often recommend to my clients for developing a vision for their lives.

- **Imagine your future self:** Write a short story or a scene from a play describing who you are, what you have accomplished, and how you are living and working in five, ten, or twenty years from now.

- **Design a vision board:** Gather magazines, cut out pictures and words that express how you see yourself in the future, and paste them on a large piece of paper. What activities, roles, people, places, and things do you want to be a part of your life? How do you want to feel about yourself, your work, and your accomplishments at that time in the future?

- **Write a 2020 job description:** Define the professional role you would like to see yourself filling in some years in the future. What are your responsibilities? What is the impact you are having on your company, your community, and the world?

- **Create a one, three, five, or ten-year plan:** State important personal and professional accomplishments that you would like to tackle in the specified time frame.

You can use any one of the previous methods to identify and shape your personal and/or professional vision (or even some other method you have read elsewhere or thought of on your own). The goal here is to find a process that excites you and feels right to you.

Dealing With the Voice of the Critic

As you are going through this process of creating a vision, beware that a little critical voice or "gremlin" might pop into your head and try to tell you all the reasons why you will not be able to accomplish your vision or why you should not go after this particular vision. I want to encourage you to send the critical voice or gremlin away during the vision-creation process (adios!) so you can really get to the heart of what your ideal work–life balance might look like. There will be plenty of time later, as you set priorities, to align your vision with reality. For now, just enjoy the process of imagining what you want your ideal work and life to look like. And keep in mind that with any type of major (or even minor) life change, the voice of the "critic" or the gremlin might pop up, saying things like, "I've been doing things this way for so long, how can I (or why) change now?" When this happens to my clients, I encourage them to lower the volume of the voice or gremlin by focusing on what is important to them now—the actions and changes they are currently formulating.

 Know What's Important: Take some time now to contemplate your own personal and professional vision and to write it down in your *7 Keys Workbook and Journal* or other dedicated work space. As you engage in this process, note that the time frame you select for your vision is up to you.

Some people prefer shorter term, others longer. For example, your shorter term vision might be, "by the end of the year I'd like to be volunteering three hours a week at a local animal shelter and taking my full four weeks of vacation rather than letting any of my vacation time expire."

Alternately, your longer term vision might be, "by my fiftieth [or sixtieth] birthday, I want to have my own successful business, volunteer ten hours a week at a local animal shelter, and take five weeks of vacation."

Regardless of a short-term or long-term vision, you will ultimately set your priorities to support your vision and then work to put those priorities into action in a desired time frame. Whichever time frame you select, aim to be as specific as possible. Being specific gives you clear targets for which to aim and increases your chances for success. Of course, you might need to formulate your vision in a general way first, such as, "by the end of the year I'd like to be more engaged in helping the community and more relaxed at work," but once you have formulated a general vision, you will want to revise it to be more specific and thus more achievable.

◆ ◆ ◆

In sum, creating your personal and/or professional vision will provide you with a road map for creating your priorities.

Developing Your Priorities

Once you have developed your personal and professional vision (no small feat!), you will be ready to start thinking about which specific priorities you want to set for yourself to achieve your larger vision. In other words, you will be ready to take the "big picture" of your vision and break it into manageable tasks, goals, and actions.

I recommend that as you go through this priority-setting process, you base it on a six-month time frame. I am not saying that you will be implementing your *entire* vision in the next six months. That could be quite overwhelming—especially if you chose one of those lofty visions like achieving world peace! Instead, I am asking you to decide the tasks, goals, and activities to which you are willing to commit in the next half of the year to *work toward your vision*. In other words, you will be selecting actionable items that reflect what is important in your vision and that help you move closer to making your vision a reality.

 Know Your Priorities: Once you are comfortable with the vision you have developed (see the *Know What's Important* fieldwork earlier in this chapter), take out your *7 Keys Workbook and Journal* or other dedicated work space (e.g., spiral notebook, personal journal, computer document, etc.) and write down a list of the tasks, goals, and activities to which you are willing to commit in the next six months to move closer to your vision.

For example, if part of your professional vision is "to advance to a leadership role in my current company," a professional priority to focus on over the next six months might be to "find a mentor to assist me in further developing my leadership skills" or "complete Project X on time, under budget, with high client satisfaction ratings." Similarly, if part of your personal vision is "to develop a healthy lifestyle while contributing to my community," a personal priority to focus on over the next six months might be to "get to the gym two to three times per week" or to "research, select, and join one volunteer opportunity that excites me."

As you go about generating the tasks, goals, and actions that you feel will best support your vision, this is the time to be realistic about the things to which you are capable of committing and achieving in the next six months. Although I want to encourage you to stretch outside of your comfort zone when designing your priorities since this is the only way that growth can happen, I also want you to set yourself up for success. Thus, things to consider as you set realistic and achievable priorities might be any of the following.

- What will your financial resources allow in the next six months?
- What kind of time resources will you have to support these priorities in the next six months?
- What will your anticipated energy level in the next six months support?
- Are you ready and willing to make the necessary adjustments in your life to implement these priorities in the next six months?

You may discover that your answers to these questions affect the kind of tasks, goals, and actions to which you commit in the coming months. For example, if you look at your finances and realize that most of your extra income right now is slated for a home renovation, you may defer your "sign up for a graduate class" action item until six months from now when the home renovation is done. Alternately, you might choose to defer the home renovation for now and apply your extra financial resources toward your schooling.

◆　◆　◆

So, the process of developing priorities will require you to make careful choices about what matters most to you. (Remember, you cannot do it all!) Once you have clearly defined what is *most* important to you, you will then be able to make more deliberate decisions when faced with demands on your time. Of course, you may choose to do other things besides and beyond your priorities from time to time, due to a life or work necessity, but you will be doing so from a conscious place and based on a sound foundation of your vision and priorities.

Using a Planning Process

For many of us, even if we have clarity regarding our vision and priorities, there is often a disconnect between knowing our priorities and doing something with that knowledge. Here is an example to consider.

> Andrew is a high school principal in a large, urban school district. His top priorities are to improve his school, engage his students, and develop his teachers. Yet, Andrew typically finds himself engaging in tasks and activities that do not support these priorities in a fundamental way. By 9:00 a.m., he has usually fielded twenty phone calls from dissatisfied parents, been interrupted ten times to deal with student crises and teacher concerns, and responded to emails from supervisors, colleagues, community members, and government officials in between whatever else might arise. Even as his day comes to a close, Andrew has not engaged in work supportive of his top priorities. As a result, he often feels depleted and demoralized and is left wondering whether he can make the impact on his school that he believed he could before he took the job.

Although Andrew knows his priorities, it is a rare day when he has more than thirty minutes to spend developing and implementing them in any formal manner. Instead, he is constantly reacting to problems as they arise, when he would benefit so much more from using his time in a *planned* way.

To gain the ability to implement his priorities, Andrew needs a planning process—he needs to come up with a method that allows him to make a choice about what *he* wants to do each day. With his current way of operating, the unplanned situations that arise and the needs of others are driving how he spends his very valuable time, instead of his priorities driving how he is spending his time.

Without a planning process in place, external factors can easily disrupt your best intentions, as was the case for Andrew. Although it can feel counterintuitive, to *gain the time* needed to pursue your priorities, you first need to *take some time* from your day to plan. By taking time up front to plan your days and weeks, you will gain the ability to stay the course of pursuing your priorities rather than getting distracted or reacting to real-time situations as Andrew did.

Let's take a look at how Andrew managed to incorporate a planning process into his day.

> Once Andrew realizes that he has set his priorities but is not actually implementing them, he decides to take the first 20 minutes of each morning as sacred planning time. During this time, his assistant will not allow him to be interrupted (unless it is a life-or-death situation that he has clearly defined). He has also let his colleagues and staff know about his planning time and is asking for their support in maintaining it. He sees this planning time as needed in order to start his day off in an ordered way. Armed with his priorities for the day, Andrew can then determine what *he* wants to do and how each action he makes is related to his priorities of the day. He is aware that he will still have to take care of crises and problems, but he will also be making time each day for meaningful progress, too.

Let's look at one more example of using a planning process to make sure that priorities get implemented. Catherine, an executive coach, represents an example of someone who is skilled at using planning time to make sure her priorities get implemented.

> Catherine builds both professional and personal planning time into her life. Professionally, Catherine meets once a month for three hours with two of her colleagues for a "Business Success Partnership." During this time, she and her partners address how they are progressing on their business goals, what is working, what is not working, and where they want to focus for the next month. They also support each other with check-ins during the month to see how they are moving toward their goals. In addition, each Sunday night, Catherine and her husband sit down with their calendars, discuss what is important to each of them and to their family that week, and how they will support each other in making those priorities happen. For example, to meet her professional priorities of the month, Catherine blocks out four hours each week over the next month to develop and market a new service she wants to offer her clients. Also, she and her husband negotiate child care responsibilities so she can attend an evening yoga class and he can play softball while getting their children to their activities as well.

By using a regular planning process, Catherine is able to implement the priorities she has set for herself: continuing to expand her business, maintaining her physical fitness, and spending time with her children.

As with creating your personal and professional vision, there are many different ways to implement a planning process. In the case of Andrew, he likes to begin each day with a planning session, while Catherine finds weekly and monthly planning sessions to be sufficient. How will you set aside time each day and/or week for planning time?

What's Your Plan? Take some time to identify what kind of planning process you would like to use to help you maintain your priorities. The following bulleted prompts are provided to help you create a viable planning process. I recommend that you complete these statements in your *7 Keys Workbook and Journal* or other dedicated work space.

- Each day I will plan in this way ...
- Each week I will plan in this way ...
- Changes I need to make, or support I need to get, in order to integrate planning into my day and week are ...

As you create your planning process, aim to be as specific as possible. For example, try to define how much time you will commit to planning each day and week, where you will be when you are using your planning time, and how you will ensure that your planning time remains sacred, meaning that this time will be uninterrupted and not rescheduled. Being specific ("I will implement my planning process this way ...") will give you a structure to which to commit, and it will also allow you to see your progress ("I just spent thirty minutes planning my week").

Note that you may need to change your current behavior and routines to implement your planning process, as well as to enlist support from others. Toward this effort, think about who and what can help you make this a reality. For example, if your office life runs at breakneck speed and is constantly full of interruptions, you may need to leave your office for planning time. If your partner or spouse is not usually a planner, you will need to ask him or her to respect your new way of operating as you implement your planning processes.

In the end, your planning process will be very personal, from creating "to-do" lists and updating calendars to writing marketing and business plans. You will select the time of day or night, interval, frequency, and methods that feel most comfortable, given your energy, style, and personality. If it feels like you are implementing someone else's planning process, you will likely not maintain it. Like your favorite pair of jeans, you want your planning process to fit well.

◆ ◆ ◆

After you have created a planning process, you will have the time and space you need to actually *create a plan* to implement your priorities over the coming days and weeks. In particular, during your planning time, you will be recording and committing to the tangible tasks, goals, and actions (which you recorded in the *Know Your Priorities* fieldwork earlier in this chapter) that support your priorities. You might also use your planning time to further develop, refine, or even revisit your priorities.

Also note that your planning may be tactical (i.e., what you want to do to reach your priorities) or strategic (i.e., what you need to think about to reach your priorities), or both. For example, tactical planning may include listing clients you need to call and vendors you need to email in order to get information to finish a report. Strategic planning may require you to set aside a few hours during the following week to decide the direction you believe is best for your department to take over the next year in response to a new competitor in your region.

The goal here is to break down your priorities into smaller, scheduled time chunks, enabling you to ultimately move from the envisioning and planning stage to the action stage.

Managing Low-Priority Creep

With your vision in place, and a planning process operational, there is still one more important aspect to becoming skilled at prioritization: managing *low-priority creep*.

Using Your Planning Time to Define Your Priorities

When you sit down for your first planning session, take some time to define your priorities in terms of a weekly or daily time frame. If you are looking at a daily time frame, select two or three priorities; for a weekly time frame, you would want to select three or four.

For example, if you are selecting a daily planning process, start by choosing one personal and one professional priority to act on each day based on your vision. This might mean during your Monday planning time, you choose to schedule time for three important marketing phone calls and make an appointment to meet a friend at the gym at 7:30 p.m.

If you are planning weekly, you may prefer to set aside planning time on Sunday evenings. During this time, while reviewing your vision and what you want to accomplish in the next six months, you may choose the following professional actions for the week—block out three half-hour time slots for reading the latest pharmaceutical industry journal and schedule an hour to plan sales meetings for the week. Your personal planning for the week may include making arrangements for a Saturday "date night" and scheduling time for training for an upcoming 10K race.

By creating a tangible plan for when and how you will be enacting the tasks, goals, and activities that support your priorities, you will take a significant step forward on your path to work–life balance.

No, managing low-priority creep is not about getting better at dealing with a person you used to date! Instead, low-priority creep is another challenge to the process of prioritization. It occurs when tasks, activities, and goals that are unimportant or less important to you than your priorities get thrown onto your path and compete for your time and energy.

Low-priority creep can occur even when you have clarity on your vision and a process in place for planning because, although you are clear on your priorities for the day, week, and beyond, you do not live and work in a vacuum. Competing interests can easily derail your desired prioritization plans. Tasks with much lower priority can easily leapfrog ahead of your top priorities if you do not have awareness of and discipline in addressing other pulls on your time.

There are a number of behaviors that make it easy for low-priority creep to take over and pull you away from your priorities. They include reacting, firefighting, and doing too much.

Reacting. When you are in a *reacting mode*, you are on autopilot with your actions. You immediately react to situations instead of deliberately deciding when to move ahead with a concern, project, or requirement. Reacting is doing just about anything that occurs when it occurs without thinking, planning, or choosing a response. This might include replying to an email because it just arrived in your inbox or answering the phone while you are in the middle of an important project with an approaching deadline.

Oftentimes, reacting causes you to jump to doing something unimportant or low-priority and then to get sidetracked from implementing your important priorities. These low priorities might be your own or others'; either way, they creep into your day and threaten to undermine your plans to implement your most important priorities.

Here is an example of reacting.

Paige is an attorney in a small family law practice, where she works on multiple cases of her own, serves as an expert on other of the Firm's cases, and works closely with the Firm's two Partners. Most of Paige's days begin with a detailed to-do list of what she wants to accomplish at work before she goes home to her family each evening. Yet, most days do not turn out as she planned. Both Partners, who value Paige's expertise, regularly interrupt Paige's time at her desk with requests for advice, resources, and strategy for handling other cases. She usually drops everything to assist the Partners and returns to her own work feeling frustrated, angry, and behind schedule.

Paige's situation shows her in a reacting mode. When her bosses or colleagues want something from her, she stops whatever she is doing to provide what they need, regardless of her own needs and priorities.

There is a simple technique to address reacting, and it only requires a breath! That is, by stopping to take a breath when a low-priority item "creeps" across her desk, Paige will be able to stay on top of her top priorities and avoid letting lower priorities take over her day.

Let's examine this technique more. First, we need to define the stimulus of the situation. In this case, it is a Partner knocking on Paige's office door with a request. Her standard reaction is to drop her task at hand in order to immediately address the Partner's request. To change her reaction to a response, though, Paige needs to take a breath after the defined stimulus (the Partner's request). This breath allows Paige to turn off the autopilot of jumping to meet the Partner's need and to create some space to evaluate when is the best time to take care of the Partner's request as well as her own work.

Paige's new response might look like the following.

"Hi, Alex. Thanks for stopping by and letting me know what's happening with the Kramer case." [She then takes a conscious, three-second breath while she reviews her priorities.] "I understand what you need and its importance. I want you to be aware of what I'm working on now and that I have a deadline in an hour. I'm happy to help out and will be in touch as soon as I complete this other document."

Of course, we do not know how Paige's boss Alex will react; but Paige has shifted her normal mode of *reacting* to one of assertively responding to her boss and engaging him in a conversation, beginning with a focus on her immediate needs and priorities. Alex may override her plans, or he may be comfortable waiting for Paige to complete her current priority. If Paige had not crafted the previous response, she would never have had the opportunity to discuss her preferred way for everyone to move ahead.

One more point to note in this example is that Paige was not defensive or aggressive with her boss. For example, she did not complain that she was finishing work he had given her yesterday and did not exclaim that her work was more important than his. She simply asserted her needs to Alex so he had some valuable information and so that they could deliberately and collectively negotiate each of their priorities.

Take some time now to consider situations in which you tend to react. Are there certain people that cause you to jump into action (or reaction)? Are there common requests that tend to make you switch gears without thinking? By identifying in which situations and with which people you have a tendency to react, you will be able to take a breath when that stimulus occurs and then choose a preferred response.

Firefighting. When you are in a *firefighting* mode, you find yourself dealing with problems (your own or others') rather than your priorities. As urgent situations occur, you immediately address them without consideration of other important priorities you have planned for the day or week. While some situations do need to be dealt with immediately (i.e., are truly urgent), others can be deferred for a period of time while you finish implementing a priority. Other situations can even be handed off to someone else in your organization or life.

School principal Andrew, mentioned earlier, often found himself firefighting. That is, before he implemented a planning process, he spent the first 3 hours of his workday handling dissatisfied parents, student crises, and teacher concerns. None of this time was spent planning or engaging in his actual priorities. To become more successful at implementing his priorities, Andrew created a planning process. However, Andrew needed to do more than simply plan his day if he wanted to succeed at prioritization. He also needed to avoid falling into firefighting mode when a situation arose that was not urgent or that someone else in the school could handle. If he managed to stay away from firefighting relatively unimportant or low-priority issues when possible, Andrew would have more ability to stay on task with his important or high priorities.

Doing too much. A final cause for low-priority creep is *doing too much*. Doing too much involves taking on more tasks, goals, and activities than you can physically or mentally complete in a given time frame. In the context of low-priority creep, doing too much involves allowing low-priority activities to crowd your time. (As we will discuss in future chapters, doing too much can also interfere with your ability to use other keys to work–life balance, such as creating boundaries and designing reasonable expectations.)

Here is an example of doing too much.

> Rachel was a global sales manager, supervising a staff of fifteen sales representatives. Her main responsibility was developing and overseeing the sales strategy for her products across the world and leading her very capable team to do their jobs. Her challenge

was that she also loved the direct contact with clients and engaging in direct sales, which was no longer her responsibility. Her direct reports knew that she loved the sales work, so they would often go to her with very minor issues and ask for her guidance, and her response was often to do things for her team, which ultimately took her away from her bigger picture responsibilities. This often left Rachel feeling behind and overwhelmed on the requirements her boss needed, so that she always felt she was working in a catch-up mode. The shift Rachel needed to make was to step back and evaluate the best use of her time within the framework of her primary responsibilities. This required her to empower her staff to do more, and for her to set limits on her availability relating to low-priority tasks that her staff could do quite effectively.

In Rachel's situation, there were definite priorities that needed to be addressed, most importantly, supporting her sales team to become more effective and therefore reach and surpass their sales goals. Yet, Rachel could support her team without actually doing their work for them. In fact, by doing less for her team she would be allowing them to grow and develop. Equally important, by clearing some low-priority tasks off her desk, Rachel could be more focused, strategic, and impactful with her main job responsibilities—her professional priorities.

As you are thinking about managing low-priority creep—whether due to reacting, firefighting, or doing too much—here are some techniques to support you. These techniques, which augment some of the ideas discussed in the *Using a Planning Process* section, can also support your overall ability to put your priorities in action.

- *Create sacred time each day or each week for important work.* This means actually scheduling uninterrupted time to focus on what really matters to you—and by scheduling this time, it means giving the same level of importance as a meeting with a client, your boss, or someone on your staff.

- *Create a process for "triaging" emergencies.* Fires *will* develop. Determine a method for evaluating what you must take care of, what someone else can take care of, and what is not your business. You will also want to have a support structure and resources to assist you in this process.

- *Create a list of projects that you are working on daily, weekly, and monthly* (and longer term if needed) that you regularly check. Develop a repeatable routine to evaluate and revisit how you are progressing with your projects.

- *Set time aside daily and/or weekly for planning and strategic thinking.* This needs to go in your calendar, diary, or PDA. If you need to, create a name for this meeting to make it feel important in your schedule such as: Appointment with M.E., Planning Meeting, Strategic Thinking Meeting—whatever will help you raise the level of importance of this time and keep the space open for you.

Now that you have an understanding of what low-priority creep is, I would like to offer you an exercise to help you tune into areas where low-priority creep may be getting in the way of your ability to implement your priorities. This exercise is also useful in assessing how you are doing overall in managing priorities and is the last exercise in this chapter.

Priorities in Action: Over the next week, try to pay attention to how you implement—or to what gets in the way of implementing—your priorities. Are you letting low-priority creep get in the way, allowing your own lesser priorities or other people's priorities to throw you off of your plan? Or maybe your planning process is broken? Did you remember to take time each day to confirm and commit to your priorities, or did you cancel your planning time in favor of some other "more important" activity? As you move into this observation phase, consider all of the things you are doing well to help you manage your priorities as well as the variety of things that may be preventing you from acting on your priorities.

In particular, take time each day or evening in the next week to ask yourself the following questions and record the answers in your *7 Keys Workbook and Journal* or other dedicated work space.

- How did I implement my priorities today?
- Am I satisfied with what I accomplished today? Why or why not?
- What can I do differently tomorrow?

As you review these questions each day or each night, if you are satisfied with your prioritization, acknowledge what worked for you and celebrate! If you are not satisfied, define what you would have liked to do differently and come up with a way to address the issue the following day, keeping your challenges with prioritization in mind, and the accompanying remedies. The goal for this exercise is to develop an ability to prioritize, choose, and evaluate ... and then repeat.

As you make time and space to prioritize your actions, you will likely feel more productive, focused, and impactful. You will be doing what is important to you, on your terms and using your best skill sets—and, if you need to respond to something that is not your priority, you will do so in a deliberate manner, making an informed choice.

By using the prioritization key—that is, by developing, implementing, and maintaining your priorities—you will be taking a powerful step toward your preferred work–life balance.

POSTCARD *from the* road

- A priority is a goal, task, or action that takes precedence and that is of significant importance, compared to other goals, tasks, or actions.
- Priorities are critical to work–life balance because you cannot do it all!
- Skilled prioritization involves developing a personal and professional vision, using a planning process, and managing low-priority creep.
- Having a defined vision enables you to know what is important to you and to make appropriate choices to support that vision.
- You can extrapolate your professional and personal priorities from your vision.
- A defined and implemented planning process gives you time each day to confirm you are acting on your vision and making choices in a manner that reflects your priorities.
- Low-priority creep occurs when nonpriorities are addressed before priorities and without your awareness or choice.
- Examples of low-priority creep include reacting, firefighting, and doing too much.
- Solutions for low-priority creep include taking a breath to get off autopilot, differentiating between urgent and important, and focusing on doing what you do best.

KEY 2

Create Boundaries

On your journey toward work–life balance, you will be engaging in an interesting game of "push–pull." On the one hand, you will be really "going for it" (that's the push part), asking of life all that you hope for and imagine for yourself: perhaps a career that you love, personal time outside of work that fulfills and rejuvenates you, connections to your community that give your life meaning, and so on—whatever unique blend of activities and associations will come together to help you feel satisfied with your life as a whole. On the other hand, you will be learning how and where and when to pull back—when to ask less of yourself, when to give less of yourself, and where to cut back.

As we saw in the previous chapter on developing priorities, you cannot do it all. To get the whole package—the entire life of which you dream—ironically, you also have to be willing to give some things up, too. The good news is that this sort of discipline is usually not about giving up the things that you love but instead about giving up things that you do not love (or like less) but have not had the clarity or strength or self-discipline to give up.

The process of developing priorities that we covered in the previous chapter is meant to help you bring to light all the things you *do* want from your life (there is that push part again) so you can add them to your schedule in the form of doable tasks, goals, and actions. The process of creating boundaries, which is the focus of the present chapter, is meant to help you discover (or rediscover!) those areas in your life in which you need to pull back to make sure you have the time, energy, and other resources needed to bring forth your ideal work–life balance.

As you become more and more skilled at creating and maintaining your boundaries, you may become amazed at the level of mental and even physical energy you are able to sustain throughout the day. It is much easier to engage in doing things that move you closer to fulfilling your priorities than to force yourself to engage in activities that support other peoples' priorities or that simply do not fulfill you. This is not to say that the journey of working toward what you want will not take hard work. It will, but it will be the kind of hard work that feels good—like hiking up to the top of a mountain that promises a beautiful view and has lovely rest points along the way.

Developing Awareness of the Key

A Closer Look at the Concept

You have probably heard of boundaries before, but let's review to be clear on the concept. *Boundaries* are limits that you set for yourself that allow you to meet your needs, maintain your priorities, and protect your values. Boundaries also include limits that you set for others in how they interact with you. For most people, maintaining basic boundaries gives some sense of control to their day as well as relief that there is a beginning and end to their work and other responsibilities.

Some examples of boundaries include the following.

- When my office door is shut, do not interrupt me (unless it is a life-or-death situation or a medical emergency).
- I do not work after 3:00 p.m. on Fridays.
- I do not answer work phone calls or email on Saturday or Sunday.
- I can only contribute two hours per week to community volunteering.
- I will respond to your email or voicemail within thirty-six hours.
- I will not take my laptop or Blackberry on vacation with me.
- I will not miss my child's school performance.
- Each week, I will try to spend some quality time with my husband and son. (This boundary is what I call a loose boundary; to be most effective, it will need to be tightened. We will revisit this topic later in the chapter.)

Boundaries protect important things in your life, including your time, your energy, your focus, your weekends, and your relationships. Boundaries also protect those priorities discussed in the previous chapter—your workout, your reading time, your quality time with your mate or kids, your professional development, your entrepreneurial interests ... whichever priorities you have chosen for yourself and whichever professional goals and personal activities matter most to you.

Boundaries are critical to greater work–life balance as they provide a structure for allowing you to maintain your priorities. If you have predefined actions that are acceptable and not acceptable for you (i.e., if you have created boundaries for yourself), you will find it easier to make choices that align with your desired work–life balance.

Because boundaries represent limits, maintaining your boundaries essentially involves saying "no," whether to yourself or others. Many people find that saying "no" to someone else feels like a high hurdle, whether to a direct report, colleague, supervisor, friend, or family member.

There are all kinds of reasons it can be hard to say "no." Maybe you do not want to let others down, hurt someone else's feelings, appear incompetent, or miss out on something. Yet, saying "no" will be much easier if you are clear on your boundaries, as you will have a defined benchmark by which to measure requests. These benchmarks make saying "no" much less personal as the decision is about something you have already determined, not about the person to whom you are saying "no." Similarly, having preset boundaries will make it easier for you to say "no" to your own tendency to take on too much—that is, to resist the temptation to squeeze one more task into your day and in the process sabotage your plans for implementing your priorities.

Let's look at an example of boundary-setting and how it helps Alison, an IT manager at a biotech company, maintain her priorities and overall work–life balance.

A colleague of Alison's asked her whether she would be willing to chair a committee for an IT professional association. Alison was flattered that her colleague saw her as a valuable contributor to the profession, and, yet, Alison was also challenged with spending quality time with her two young children and husband, fulfilling her many work and nonwork commitments, and pursuing her master's degree. Fortunately, Alison had already set boundaries for herself. As a result, in response to her colleague's request, Alison replied, "Thanks for considering me for this opportunity. It means a lot to me that you think I could contribute to the association. Unfortunately I can't do this now, as my professional development time is fully booked. Not sure if you are aware I'm working toward my master's degree and taking two graduate classes at night. This might be something I could consider after I graduate."

In this example, Alison has a well-defined boundary. Besides her work and family time, she has committed to further professional development by completing an advanced degree. To obtain this, she evaluated her time and felt she could do this by putting aside ten hours a week—four hours for classes and six additional hours for reading and homework. During the two years of her degree program, she decided not to take on any additional professional development activities outside of work hours, so there would be no further infringement on her nonwork priorities. Because she is very clear on her availability and willingness regarding this component of her time, saying "no" was just a matter of recalling this boundary and graciously declining her colleague's inquiry.

In the previous example, Alison has a clear understanding of when she needs to set up a boundary (i.e., to say "no") in order to protect how she wants to spend her time. This clarity simplifies her decision-making process, making it straightforward, easy, and efficient.

In sum, boundaries are limits you have created for yourself that help you say "no" to things like opportunities, tasks, responsibilities, and requests in order to support your desired work–life balance.

Identifying the Barrier: Lack of Personal and Professional Boundaries

People who are not well skilled at setting or maintaining boundaries struggle with the barrier of *lack of personal and professional boundaries*. People facing this barrier have absent boundaries, loose boundaries, or some combination of both. *Absent boundaries* refer to situations in which you have not put any limits in place to protect something that is important to you. *Loose boundaries* refer to cases in which you have some desired boundary in mind but this boundary is not currently functioning effectively, because of one of the following reasons.

- The boundary is too general or unspecific.
- You have trouble communicating the boundary to others.
- You have trouble enforcing the boundary.

Here are some examples of loose and absent boundaries (as noted in the parentheses).

- You bring your laptop on vacations in order to keep up with the office. (Absent)
- Your PDA feels like part of the family; it is with you more than your partner or children when at home. (Absent)
- You can't say "no" to a supervisor, peer, or direct report. (Absent)
- You are unwilling to say "no" to acquaintances, friends, or family. (Absent)
- You always put others' preferences before your own. (Absent)

- You allow yourself to always be available for unscheduled meetings. (Absent)
- You rarely leave your office before 7:30 p.m. on most nights. (Loose)
- You arrive late to your evening exercise class because a conference call ran later than scheduled. (Loose)
- You postpone your dentist appointment again as your boss needed to speak with you just as you were heading out the door. (Loose)
- You take on one more project because your colleague says it will be the last time she asks for your help. (Loose)

In some of these cases, there are no boundaries at all, such as when you always say "yes" to a supervisor. In other cases, the boundaries are loose, such as when you are regularly late for personal appointments or activities due to a work commitment.

Jonathan, a human resources professional at a large consulting firm, represents someone who is unable to maintain boundaries.

Jonathan is responsible for supporting a group of 400 employees for all of their HR needs, and he also manages a very high-profile technology project for his division. He reports directly to two different HR leaders and has dotted-line reporting to another firm leader. He also is married, has two children, and is very involved in his community. In particular, he coaches his daughter's soccer team and his son's basketball team. He also serves on a local government committee, organizes an annual fundraising event for his community art center, takes ballroom dancing lessons with his wife, and plays on his synagogue's softball team. He enjoys both his work and his personal commitments, yet he always feels pulled in too many directions. People are constantly asking him to help out on more and more projects as he is so competent and committed. He yearns for some "down time" without any responsibilities, phone calls, or follow-up, but he doesn't see how it would be possible given all of his current involvements and all that he knows will continue to come his way.

Jonathan is exhibiting the barrier of lack of personal and professional boundaries. Because he has not set many limits for himself—that is, he says "yes" to nearly every opportunity that comes his way as well as to other people's many requests on his time, regardless of his time and energy—Jonathan's desired work–life balance is out of whack. He'd like more relaxed time away from all of his responsibilities, but he has not put any boundaries in place to protect this particular wish.

As a result of Jonathan's lack of boundaries, colleagues, supervisors, friends, and acquaintances constantly request and even expect Jonathan's support and assistance when they need it. This leads to frustration and annoyance for Jonathan, and also for his wife and kids, as he seems to always be busy with something and often unable to fully engage in his present situation.

Does Jonathan's situation sound familiar to you? Do you find yourself taking on nearly every request that comes your way? Is it natural for you to take care of everyone else, even at the expense of your own needs, or to get involved in every interesting opportunity around you? Do you often feel resentful of the tasks, activities, and roles for which you are currently responsible? If so, a lack of personal and professional boundaries may be preventing you from achieving your desired work–life balance.

Where Are You Using Boundaries Right Now?

Interestingly, no matter how many loose or absent boundaries you identify in yourself, you most likely already have some boundaries that you maintain. For example, if you get to your dentist's office every six months for teeth cleaning, if you pick your child up from daycare by 6:30 p.m. each night, or if you commit to joining friends for a monthly book group, you have some boundaries and are able to maintain them. In other words, you are able to say "no" to other things that could have possibly infringed on these commitments. Take some time now to reflect on—or, better yet, pull out your *7 Keys Workbook and Journal* or other dedicated work space and write down—all the areas in your life where you are already good at maintaining boundaries. At work? With your spouse or partner? With your children? In your volunteer commitments? With your friends? What allows you to keep boundaries in these areas? Is it an approach that you can transfer to other important areas of your life? Lastly, congratulate yourself for successfully maintaining boundaries in these areas!

Putting the Key Into Practice

If you are getting the sense that this particular key—the key of creating personal and professional boundaries—will help you move closer to your preferred work–life balance, I invite you to spend some time identifying your loose and absent boundaries.

Identify Your Loose and Absent Boundaries: Over the next week, try to observe how (and even if) you set boundaries. In your *7 Keys Workbook and Journal* or your dedicated work space, write down your loose or absent boundaries. For example, you might identify the following absent boundary:

I take work phone calls at all hours, including evenings and weekends.

Once you have identified a given boundary issue, take some time to write down how this particular absent or loose boundary makes you feel and what kind of impact you believe it is having on your work and life. For example, you might write ...

I never feel like I can relax and work never seems to be over. My wife gets mad that I never seem to focus on her, even when we're alone and supposed to be having fun.

By identifying your loose and/or absent boundaries and quantifying their impact, you can more clearly decide if this way of operating works for you. This will, ideally, allow you to make behavioral changes for greater work–life satisfaction.

◆   ◆   ◆

Once you have completed the process of identifying your loose and absent boundaries, you will have a useful list of the areas that make up your boundary challenges. You will then be able to draw on this list to develop a new plan for ...

- creating boundaries in the areas where they are currently absent
- tightening boundaries where they are currently loose.

The next section of the chapter will help you do both.

Creating and Tightening Boundaries

Now that you have discovered (or been reminded of!) your absent and loose boundaries, let's explore how you can go about creating meaningful boundaries that further support your priorities and give you more control over your work–life balance.

The goal here is to turn your loose and absent boundaries into firm, meaningful boundaries that allow you to focus your time and energy doing the tasks and actions that you defined as your priorities (or as steps to achieving your priorities) in the previous chapter. To do this, you need to create SMART boundaries. (You may have heard of SMART goals. Here, you will be applying the SMART concept to creating your boundaries.)

For a boundary to be effective, it must have the following characteristics. It must be ...

- **S**pecific – you can clearly define the action or lack of action you will take
- **M**easurable – you can quantify the boundary and are aware when you are or you are not doing it
- **A**ttainable – you can actually do it; it is feasible to implement this boundary
- **R**ealistic – you believe you can uphold it; it is not unmanageable or unreasonable
- **T**ime-based – you define it within a time frame.

Let's use the SMART model to turn the loose boundary shown in the following text (which was also mentioned near the start of the chapter) into a firm boundary.

Each week, I will try to spend some quality time with my husband and son.

To make this boundary firm, the following adjustments can be made.

- I can make the boundary statement more **S**pecific by changing "quality time" to "undistracted, nonmultitasking time."

- I can make it more **M**easurable by changing "Each week" to "Monday through Thursday."
- I can make it more **A**ttainable by changing "will try to spend" to "will spend."
- I can make it more **R**ealistic and **T**ime-based by changing "some quality time" to a defined amount of time (e.g., an hour and a half each evening).

As a result, the new firm boundary might appear as follows:

Monday through Thursday, I will spend undistracted, nonmultitasking time with my family—at least one hour with my son and a half hour with my husband.

To get even more specific, I might also define what I will not do:

During this time, I will not go into my home office, touch my iPhone, or look at a to-do list.

By defining what I will not do, I am making this boundary even more specific. My actions and lack-of-actions are very well defined, making it easier to implement this boundary.

In a moment, you will have an opportunity to practice taking one of your own absent or loose boundaries and making it firm—but, first, let's walk through one more example to gain more insight into what this exercise of making boundaries firm might look like in practice.

Steve, an accountant for a national furniture store, wanted to firm up the following absent boundary (described earlier):

I take work phone calls at all hours, including evenings and weekends.

As we can see, Steve had no boundaries around taking work calls. He would respond to them any time of night or day, every single day of the week. When he decided to make a firm SMART boundary around this issue, he created the following boundary statement:

> *I will not answer work-related calls or check voicemails after 7:30 p.m. on Mondays through Thursdays, or after 6:00 p.m. on Fridays through 7:00 a.m. on Mondays.*

Steve's new, firm boundary statement followed the SMART model. It was …

- **S**pecific in that he defined what he will not do (answer work-related calls or check voicemails)
- **M**easurable in that it is very clear whether he is answering a work call or not
- **A**ttainable in that he can easily turn off his cell phone, which is where he received all after-hour work calls
- **R**ealistic in that being available over twelve hours each weekday is more than enough to do his job well
- **T**ime-based in that he defined time ranges in which to answer or not answer calls.

After creating his new, firm boundary regarding when he would and would not field work-related calls, Steve needed to go one step further and commit to a plan for implementing that boundary. Here is what his plan looked like.

> *I need to let my colleagues know about this change so they can adjust the way they communicate with me. I also need to have a new place to put my mobile phone so I don't constantly look at it when it rings and then feel guilty for not answering. Or I could just turn it off most of the time. Lastly, I need to remember that none of my work is life-or-death and that I work best when I'm focused and in my office, anyway.*

After a week of implementing his boundary of not taking work-related calls at night or on weekends, Steve wrote the following text in his journal.

> *The first few days were tough. I felt like I may have been letting people down who might have needed me, or people might have perceived me as slacking on the job. What was amazing, though, was that after I got in the pattern of actually leaving my phone in my car's glove compartment, I actually felt lighter and happier to be home. My wife commented that I didn't seem as uptight after about a week and I felt like I was really paying attention to my kids, instead of waiting for the next call to come through.*

The following fieldwork exercise will guide you in a process similar to Steve's of creating firm boundaries and then reflecting on how you feel after implementing that boundary.

 Creating Firm Boundaries: Now that you have the SMART model to guide you toward success, take some time to revisit the list of absent and loose boundaries you described in the *Identify Your Loose and Absent Boundaries* fieldwork earlier in this chapter and spend some time creating a firm boundary for each absent or loose boundary. As you create each firm boundary, jot some notes down, too, on how you plan to implement the new boundary. To be effective, you will need to do this exercise in a formal way, whether in your *7 Keys Workbook and Journal* or other dedicated work space, since each firm boundary has several pieces to it and you will want to be able to refer back to these boundaries—and plans for implementation—as you practice maintaining them.

As you create a plan for implementing a particular boundary, consider the following questions. What do you need to do differently in order to maintain this boundary? To whom do you need to communicate your boundary and what do you plan to say to this person or these people?

What new, firm boundaries do you need to create in order to be able to maintain all the meaningful priorities you generated for yourself in the previous chapter? What loose boundaries do you need to tighten in order to move toward your ideal work–life balance?

Once you have rewritten a new, firm boundary to correspond with each of the absent or loose boundaries on the list you generated earlier in the chapter (*Identify Your Loose and Absent Boundaries* fieldwork), take some time to get familiar with your new boundaries. Imagine yourself upholding each of them and enjoying the benefits from implementing your new boundary-related behaviors. The more you are able to envision yourself upholding your boundaries and benefiting from them, the more natural it will become to maintain them when faced with real-life challenges on your attention and time.

Now that you have newly defined firm boundaries and are aware of what changes you need to make in order to implement them, I encourage you to choose one boundary that you believe will give you the most satisfaction to enact. Over the next week, test out this new boundary, using the plan you designed to implement it.

As you are practicing maintaining this particular boundary, reflect on the benefits of creating or tightening your first boundary and what you seem to be gaining from this implementation. I recommend that you pay attention to ...

- how you feel as you maintain this boundary
- the benefits you are gaining from maintaining this boundary.

Again, you might find it very useful to write your reflections down in your journal.

When you are comfortable maintaining this new boundary, I encourage you to choose another from your list and revisit the same process of boundary-maintaining, followed by reflection, until you have implemented all of the desired boundaries from your list.

◆ ◆ ◆

Having a specific plan for creating and maintaining your boundaries will set you up for success because you will know exactly what you need to do to prepare others to respect your boundary as well as what you need to do to make that boundary a reality. Of course, people may still try to challenge your boundary after you have communicated it to them, but you will have at least laid the groundwork for sticking to your plan.

Thoughts That Interfere With Boundary-Setting

As you try out using this particular key to work–life balance, pay attention to the counterproductive thoughts that might pop into your head, making it hard for you to use this particular key to work–life balance. Some of the more common counterproductive thoughts you might face when trying to set boundaries are described in the text that follows.

I don't want to rock the boat because the waves will make me uncomfortable. When this mode of thinking occurs, you want to employ a boundary but you are unwilling to do so because you do not want to experience the discomfort that you anticipate will come with that boundary-setting. This particular challenge comes about when you are fearful of conflict and would rather not rock the boat or create waves by asking others to respect your desired boundaries. For example, your boss often asks you to do small tasks just as you are about to leave the office. This causes you to be late (or miss) scheduled events or meaningful time with your family. You would prefer it if your boss would refrain from giving you work fifteen minutes or less before your departure time, but you are unwilling to set this boundary with her because the idea of communicating this boundary makes your shoulders tense and your heart beat faster.

When my clients are afraid to rock the boat, I encourage them to view the situation as an opportunity to design a better solution for everyone involved. Setting a boundary does not have to be negative or fear-inducing. Instead, it can lead to growth, change, and a more preferable outcome. It can also give you a chance to practice assertive communication—asking for what you want while respecting the other person's needs.

I do it because I can. When you are using this mode of thinking, you do something because you can, not because you really want to. The reason you do not set boundaries in this scenario is often because it seems more efficient not to set a boundary. For example, you have always done the grocery shopping for your family and though you would rather take this task off your weekly calendar, it feels like it would just take too much time to sit down with your spouse and ask if he or she would be willing to take over this activity or to write a list to enable your spouse to do the shopping. Another reason for doing something only because you can might be that you are seen as the expert on something and feel badly leaving others without your support. For example, everyone in the office always asks you to fix the copier when it gets jammed because you are so good at it. Even though you would rather spend your time focusing on tasks important to you, you help out because you can and because you do not want to let other people down.

When my clients fall into the trap of doing something because they can, I encourage them to quantify what is the better use of their time. I also encourage them to consider what they (and their organization or others) would gain by acting on that better use of time. Once the value of their time has been quantified, it is often easier for my clients to communicate the boundary (or preferred behavior) for that situation.

Everyone else manages to do it, so why shouldn't I? In this case, you and others see yourself as the ultimate team player, and you pride yourself in that role; setting boundaries seems incongruent with how you are and like to be seen. For example, the company you work at deeply values collaboration and teamwork, and all of the work you do is project based, so you are always interacting on and with a team. You love the camaraderie, creativity, and connections of your work and are fortunate to work with great people, who are as committed to their work as you are. Still, you would really like to cut back on your sixty-hour work weeks so you have some time to pursue at least one of your hobbies. Yet, you won't set boundaries to make that happen because you do not want to seem like a slacker.

In this kind of a situation, I encourage my clients to do a few things. First, review the evidence of your performance. My hunch is that if you are committed to being a collaborator and team player, even cutting back some of your hours will not impact your commitment and work ethic. Second, remember that not everyone on a team needs to contribute in exactly the same manner. Your strengths and skills will be used best when you are at your best. Finally, experiment with the word "and." For example, try asking yourself whether you can be a team player *and* also have more manageable hours. These two factors do not have to be mutually exclusive. Sometimes we assume others will think less of us if we set boundaries, but often they want to do the same thing and are also fearful of making a change. By setting boundaries and maintaining them, you can actually be a role model for others. Of course, some people may judge you for setting boundaries. If that does happen, you can decide what is more important—other people's opinions or moving toward your more preferred work–life balance.

I could lose something, instead of gain. When you use this mode of thinking, you fear that others will react negatively to your boundary-setting (i.e., be resentful, angry, unsupportive) or that there will be undesirable consequences in response to your boundary-setting. For example, you might worry that your professional path may be limited or questioned if you set boundaries, so you avoid setting them.

For clients who do not set boundaries because they worry about the negative consequences, I remind them that they can experiment with this process and take small steps toward setting boundaries. As you take one step in setting a boundary (like letting your boss know you cannot work past 6:30 p.m. on Wednesday nights), you can gauge any possible concerns along the way and make adjustments. If you also communi-cate your boundaries by stating your personal needs (and not judging or making demands of others), most likely, all par-ties involved will respect your choices. And, if you do notice any negative consequences, you can choose to not set a specific boundary, to change it, or to get feedback from the person(s) involved to understand any concerns.

Why bother? In this scenario, you may be thinking, "When setting boundaries, I'm sure to break the boundary, so why bother setting it in the first place?" In other words, you think that there is no point in setting a boundary unless you can always maintain it. Yet, boundary-setting does not have to be so rigid. As I will discuss later in the chapter, boundaries can be flexible, meaning that you can make choices about when to let them down temporarily.

When my clients struggle with the "why bother?" syn-drome, I encourage them to think about the value of having the boundary structure in place to help them make deliberate choices regarding how they spend their time. That is, if my clients already have a boundary in place, it is much easier for them to let down that boundary temporarily than it is to have no boundary in place and then try to say "no" on the spot in a given situation.

So, there are a number of reasons why people struggle to define, communicate, and maintain boundaries. Some people believe it is not worth it—that they will lose more than they gain—other people worry that they will be seen as slacking, and still others are uncomfortable challenging the status quo.

Define Your "Buckets"

A powerful antidote to the thoughts that might pop up as you try to set boundaries is something I call *buckets*. Buckets are imaginary or symbolic containers for how you want to spend your time. Knowing your buckets—the important areas in which you want to spend your time each week—will make it easier for you to say "no" (to set boundaries) because you are very certain as to where you want to say "yes."

To conduct this optional exercise, think of your time each week as a finite quantity of sand that needs to be put in buckets. Each bucket represents a defined way in which you want to spend your time. You get to decide the size of each bucket and the number of buckets that you have—but the total volume of all of the buckets needs to equal the total quantity of sand. You can choose not to fill all of your buckets, but they cannot overflow. In other words, you have a limited and defined amount of time each week. In what ways do you want to spend that time?

Here are examples of my buckets:

> *Bucket 1: Time With My Husband and Son*
> *Bucket 2: Coaching and Business Time*
> *Bucket 3: Yoga and Exercise Time*
> *Bucket 4: Piano Time*
> *Bucket 5: Taking Care of the House and Family*
> *Bucket 6: Time with Friends*
> *Bucket 7: Unscheduled/Down Time*

I am involved with many other activities, but these are the major areas to which I know I want to commit time each week. I also want to be sure that some time is not planned. Knowing the important areas in which I want to spend my time each week—my buckets—will make it easier for me to say "no" as I am very certain as to where I will say "yes."

What are your buckets? Create a list of all the buckets you would like to fill in your life. For inspiration on the kind of buckets you would like to create, you may want to return to the priorities you developed for yourself in the previous chapter (*Know Your Priorities* fieldwork).

Tighten Up, Then Lighten Up

One final concept to consider when implementing a new boundary is the idea of "tighten up, then lighten up." In other words, plan on creating and tightening all of your boundaries where needed (as identified earlier in the chapter), and only then becoming flexible—when and where you determine it to be appropriate. The reason for this approach is that it is always easier to lessen a firm boundary than to tighten a loose one. So, as you experiment with your new boundaries, I recommend that you start very firmly. If you need to, you can always loosen your boundaries if that feels more comfortable to you. But start by doing all of the hard work first; later, you can tweak your boundaries, if needed, to work for you and your desired situation.

Here is an example of the "tighten up, then lighten up" concept in action.

> In an attempt to get her unwieldy work hours under control, Molly finally decides to *set a boundary* around the time she is able to commit to work. She decides that she will leave her office on Mondays, Wednesdays, and Fridays by 6:30 p.m. She recognizes that she will almost always have additional work to do as her day comes to a close, given the nature of her work as a medical editor for a publishing company, but Molly chooses to set this boundary because she believes she will return to work more refreshed the following day and will be a better employee over the long-term if she leaves the office some days in time to have a quick dinner and a swim (which she can only accomplish by leaving work at 6:30 p.m.).

To implement this new boundary, Molly sets up a meeting with her boss. She lets him know that due to some new external commitments, she will need to leave the office at her desired specific times on some days each week. Molly has a great performance history, has worked for the company for over three years, and is seen as a very committed employee. As it turns out, Molly's boss is fine with this request and just asks that Molly continue to give him regular updates, especially around deadlines. She was surprised how easy it was to address her newly planned way of working.

Note a few things about Molly's situation.

- *Molly did not tell her boss the specifics of her "external commitment."* Molly was concerned that she needed to give her boss a reason for why she was leaving the office at 6:30 p.m. Then she remembered that many of her colleagues who have children often leave at a specified time each day, even earlier than 6:30 p.m., to take care of children and other family responsibilities.
- *Molly did not ask permission from her boss.* As she was already working well beyond traditional work hours and was performing well, Molly was informing her boss about her new boundary, not asking.
- *Molly acknowledged her boss's concern about deadlines.* Fortunately, Molly had never missed a deadline. She will continue to be aware of her time and efficiency around deadlines and she will be sure to communicate very clearly with her boss during these times as that was his only concern mentioned when communicating her new boundary.

- *Molly will be able to* choose *to stay later on a Monday, Wednesday or Friday, as an exception based on her choice,* not as an assumption that she is always available for whatever needs to be done. This is the "lighten up" part of the strategy. She can lessen her defined boundary on her terms, using a case-by-case decision-making process.

Now it is your turn to experiment and implement your new, firmer boundaries.

With each new boundary you maintain, your comfort level will very likely increase around boundary-setting and you are likely to find many benefits of maintaining this process. These benefits may include the following.

- You will have more clarity on the divisions between your professional and personal life, and it will be easier not to blur these two domains if you choose not to do so. You may even enjoy a vacation completely focused on vacation activities!
- You will become more comfortable turning off your technology and communication devices when it is not necessary to have them on.
- You will get more comfortable with saying "no" for work, personal, and community requests.
- You will view your preferences as being as important as (or even more important than) others' preferences.
- Your colleagues, friends, and family will show greater respect and admiration for you as you role model boundaries that make you more effective and happier. (Warning – you may also experience jealousy from some people, who wish that they could create firm, supportive boundaries, too.)

- Even if you have to make exceptions to your boundaries, you will be able to alter your boundaries instead of just disregarding them completely. Once you raise the bar in this area, you are likely to be much more careful about letting others call the shots for your time and energy.

As you can see, by taking the time and energy to create boundaries and then maintain them, you end up switching to a mode of operation that adds valuable breathing room to your day and week so you can ultimately focus on the priorities that are most important to you. That is, you *pull back* in certain areas, so you have the time and energy to *push forward* with all the priorities that will move you closer to your ideal work–life balance.

- Boundaries are limits that you set for yourself (or for others) that allow you to meet your needs, values, and priorities. Boundaries protect important things in your life.
- An obstacle to firm boundaries is the challenge of saying "no."
- Practice saying "no." It will feel easier each time you do it, especially when you start feeling the impact and benefits.
- Pay attention to your patterns around boundaries. Know when you have a tendency to let them loosen or even disappear.
- The challenging thoughts (in abbreviated form) to upholding boundaries include the following perspectives: "don't rock the boat," "I do it because I can," "everyone else manages, so why shouldn't I?", "I could lose something instead of gain," and "why bother?"
- Understand the impact of absent or loose boundaries.
- Define your new boundaries in a SMART way.
- Implement firmer boundaries one at a time. Get comfortable with the new way and then work on another.
- Remember to "tighten up, then lighten up." It is always easier to loosen a firm boundary than to tighten a loose boundary.

KEY 3

Manage Your Day Efficiently

I f you were given a piece of blank paper and a magic marker and asked to write a word for or draw a picture of every activity you wish you had time for each day or week, I suspect that in a short amount of time, you would completely fill the paper. Chances are, if you have found yourself reading this book, you have a long mental to-do list of all the things you wish you could do each week—some things for pleasure, some for peace of mind, and others to fulfill your responsibilities—but never seem to have time.

If you are feeling dissatisfied with your current work–life balance, there is a good possibility that you are feeling like you simply do not have enough time in the day to give attention to all of the things about which you care. If this is the case, you might find yourself making statements such as, "If only I had more time," "If only I needed less sleep," or "If only I could work part-time." You might find yourself wishing for some magical solution that could add more hours to your twenty-four-hour day. As you probably know all too well, though,

79

there is no magic spell that can give us more time in a day. Yet, you can, with some deliberate decision-making and some practice become more efficient and effective at managing the twenty-four hours in a day.

This chapter will guide you in a process of identifying the causes in your life for inefficient management of your day—what I call your *leaks*—and provide you with some techniques for becoming more efficient at managing your day—what I call *plugging your leaks*—so you can get the most out of the time you have in a given day.

As you may be detecting, this chapter is in large part about effective time management. But managing your day efficiently is also about managing other things, too—such as your energy, your attention, and your focus. Thus, this chapter is intended to help you manage all of these things—time, energy, and attention (or focus)—so you can ultimately get the most out of your day (i.e., spend it efficiently and in a way that meets your priorities and responsibilities) and move closer to your preferred work–life balance.

Developing Awareness of the Key

A Closer Look at the Concept

There are often leaks in people's days that lessen their productivity and take them away from their priorities, responsibilities, and to-do items. For example, Rob, a microbiologist, needs to finish a write-up of a study he and his lab partners completed yesterday. He has been sitting at his computer for ten minutes, writing a few things up, when his assistant drops a new issue of an academic journal onto his desk. Instead of staying focused on his study write-up, Rob grabs the journal and opens it. He intends to only skim the table of contents and then return to his write-up, but he ends up taking twenty minutes to read a couple of articles. Rob has just experienced a leak in his day, which has taken him away from his priority of completing his study write-up.

Leaks are defined as actions or lack-of-actions that increase demands on a person's time, energy, and/or focus and shift the person away from his or her priorities, responsibilities, or important to-do items.

In the context of the previous example, that means that instead of remaining focused on his study write-up (his priority for the day), Rob switched his focus to reading a professional journal. His leak of reading the journal ended up draining valuable time, energy, and attention that could be used to finish his study write-up on schedule.

Let's take a look at another example of someone who faces leaks in her day. Grace, a project manager at a pharmaceutical company, would like to alter her work–life balance, but she is having trouble doing so due to some serious leaks in her time, energy, and attention.

Grace oversees multiple project teams, each with four to five direct reports. Besides these supervisory responsibilities, Grace is responsible for making sure large amounts of data are accurate, which takes focus and concentration. When Grace sits at her desk reviewing data, she is typically bombarded with emails, voicemail, instant messages, and drop-in visits from her staff. She makes a practice of responding to everyone right away because she prides herself in being available and accessible to her staff. In addition, she always keeps her door open so people feel comfortable asking for her assistance. Reacting to each of these seemingly important interruptions often leaves Grace behind on her core responsibilities by the end of the day, thus requiring her to work until 9:00 p.m. most nights in the office and then to try to catch up on her 600+ emails over the weekend.

Grace's day is filled with a variety of leaks. Let's examine Grace's leaks in more detail, as they represent common leaks that many of us face.

Responding to email when it arrives. Grace reacts to the "ding" of her arriving email no matter what she is in the middle of doing. When she hears that noise, she usually stops everything and reads the incoming message. This takes her away from the immediate task that she had chosen to do.

Answering the phone while working on a project. Similar to email, Grace picks up the phone every time it rings, regardless of what she is doing. When the phone rings, she allows it to become another demand on her time, instead of protecting her current to-do item from such external factors as a call from someone else.

Having instant message on at all times. Grace keeps her instant messaging program open all day, which keeps her feeling on edge. Knowing that at any time someone might "ping" her, she never fully engages in her current projects. Since others can "see" that she is online, she feels she needs to reply to any message that comes in immediately. Like a runner on the starting blocks of a race, she feels a sense of urgency and anxiety at most times.

Keeping her door open at all times. Grace's intentions in keeping her office door open at all times are good. She wants to be available and approachable to all of her direct reports as well as her other colleagues who may need her. Yet, this open-door policy undermines her effectiveness. By keeping her door open at all times, indiscriminately allowing for a visit from someone in need or someone taking a break looking for a chat, Grace is permitting others to impact her focus and does not allow for deep concentration or prolonged work, both of which are critical to the type of work Grace needs to accomplish each day.

Working late. Grace is a morning person. She likes to be at her desk by 7:30 a.m. and feels she is at her best until 2:00 p.m. After her afternoon slump, she gets re-energized until about 6:00 p.m., when she is most often wiped out from her always intense days. She feels she needs to work until 7:00 p.m. to stay afloat, but when she works that late, she often finds mistakes the next morning, and it usually takes her twice as long to complete tasks as it does in the earlier part of the day.

If Grace's situation or any of her leaks sound familiar to you, you are not alone. Most busy professionals face a number of competing demands each day, from the different people with whom they interact to the multiple projects on their to-do list.

Although it might feel good to stay up-to-the-minute on email, will doing so sabotage your ability to complete projects that take sustained concentration? Although you may want to create a culture of openness and availability by leaving your door open every minute of every day, would your productivity benefit by shutting your office door for a few hours in the middle of the day? Using your time, energy, and attention as effectively and efficiently as possible can increase your ability to maintain work–life balance.

The next section of the chapter will provide you with an opportunity to assess whether time, energy, and attention leaks are impeding your own work–life balance and, if so, to identify what these leaks look like.

Identifying the Barrier: Inefficient Use of Time, Energy, and Attention

If you find yourself facing leaks, as Grace does, then you are facing the barrier of *inefficient use of time, energy, and attention*. This barrier, which occurs when you have difficulty managing your day efficiently, takes you away from your priorities, responsibilities, and other to-do items. In the process, you may be moving away from your desired work–life balance rather than toward it.

As shown by Grace's example, there are a variety of leaks in time, energy, and attention that can lead to this particular barrier. Many of these leaks are described in the text that follows. As you read through these leaks, think about your own life and whether any of these leaks apply to you. You might discover other leaks, not listed here, in the process, too. Knowing your leaks is the first step in minimizing and eventually stopping them.

Multitasking

Do you have a tendency (and maybe even a preference) to do more than one thing at a time? In other words, do you spend your day multitasking? Multitasking occurs when you switch from activity to activity every so many minutes instead of giving your attention to a single activity for a sustained period of time. For example, while completing a sales report, you check your email, read a few of the emails that seem important, respond to one, then go to an interesting website that was in another email, and then back to your sales report, forgetting where you were only eight minutes ago. You may feel energized while multitasking as if you are accomplishing more than if you were working on three projects separately. Unfortunately, our brains were not made to work well this way. The amount of energy it takes to switch between projects and then return to full efficiency takes more time than to work on one project, complete the required work, and then switch and fully focus on the next project.[1] If you spend your day multitasking—switching from activity to activity very frequently—you may experience a significant leak of your valuable time, energy, and attention that could be applied to better productivity.

Lack of Planning Time

Leaks in our time, energy, and attention often get created when we have not planned our days in advance. When we are busy and overwhelmed with work and life projects, it becomes particularly common to skip planning. Yet, without planning time, what we end up doing may not be what is most important

---

[1] "Cognitive Control in Media Multitaskers," 2009, by Eyal Ophira, Clifford Nass, and Anthony D. Wagner. *Proceedings of the National Academy of Sciences*, Vol. 106, No. 33.

or most efficient. When we do not plan, we usually resort to a "just do it" mode, meaning that activity trumps productivity. We falsely believe that doing anything is as good as or better than deciding the best use of our time. That is, we mistake activity for purposeful action. The idea of crossing things off a to-do list becomes more attractive then evaluating what is the best use of our time and planning to do it. (As you might recall, planning was also discussed in the *Develop Priorities* chapter.)

No Support Structure

Another leak occurs when you do not put a support structure in place to help you manage your day efficiently or when you have a support structure but do not utilize it. Support structure refers to the people and resources—such as your computer, your PDA, your administrative assistant, the company IT technician, the babysitter, and even your local drycleaner, dog walker, or online shopping service—that enable you to complete tasks.

Oftentimes, many of us assume that we need to do everything ourselves or that we need to figure everything out for ourselves. In the process, we end up taking on more than we can handle (creating leaks in our time, energy, and attention) or even recreating the wheel with each project and activity instead of using our support structure. Yet, this approach can create a significant drain of time, energy, and attention.

Who or what can help you with what you need to do? Whether at work or at home, you need to know what resources and people—what *support structure*—can undertake, enhance, or expedite what you wish to complete. Ultimately, you do not need to do everything yourself and you do not need to be the expert on everything, nor would it be beneficial or even possible to do so.

No Delegation

Whereas the leak of no support structure refers to not drawing on the *people and resources* around you that help you complete tasks, the leak of no delegation refers to not using the *skill or process* of getting the right people on your team to be doing the things that are best suited for them. When you use delegation, you enable yourself to manage your own day most efficiently, spending your time, energy, and attention on the priorities and responsibilities most important and relevant to your work and life and letting those on your team engage in the work they are best at doing. (Note that delegation is related to support structure in that the people to whom you delegate are in your support structure; but delegation is a *process* and support structure is made up of *people*—as well as *resources*.)

For many people, the thought of delegation—the process of asking someone else to do something for them—is challenging, uncomfortable, and even anxiety-producing. In reality, though, if people do not use delegation, they will not be at their best. In addition, when people forego delegation, they do not allow others around them to grow their responsibilities. Delegation actually creates a win–win situation when done appropriately.

Clutter/Messy Office or Work Space

When there is too much "stuff" in your place of work or activity, or your things are not organized well, this messiness and clutter slows you down, causing a leak in your time, energy, and attention while you search for what you need. If you are investing time in looking for papers, finding a folder or letter, or rummaging for the dry-cleaning pick-up ticket, for example, you will not be able to focus on your important task at hand, for example, leaving the house for a medical appointment. Knowing where everything you need is allows for greater efficiency. Also, an organized and functional space permits greater calmness and flow, and fewer distractions.

Social Networking Black Hole

You plan to check your Facebook account for a few minutes, revise your profile on LinkedIn, or email a friend about a video on YouTube. An hour (or three hours!) later, you realize it is now too late to do anything that you had hoped to accomplish and you are cursing yourself for the time wasted and lack of productivity. Although social networking can be a nice way to take a break and re-energize, if done without discipline, it can also create a tremendous leak of your time.

The previous leaks are common drains on time, energy, and attention at work and at home. Of course, there are other leaks, too, which you will likely discover as you contemplate drains on your own time, energy, and attention. Knowing where your leaks are will enable you to make changes to enhance your efficiency and productivity.

On that note, let's take some time now to assess your own leaks.

 Identify Your Leaks: Over the next week, look for areas in your work or personal life where you are experiencing leaks in your day. As a review, *leaks* are defined as actions or lack-of-actions that increase demands on your time, energy, and attention and that take you away from your priorities and responsibilities. Leaks can also be described as the causes in your life for inefficient use of your time, energy, or attention. They can include things like ...

- multitasking
- lack of planning
- no support structure
- no delegation
- clutter/messy office or work space
- social networking black hole.

As the week progresses, observe how efficiently or inefficiently you work and how well or how poorly you manage your time, energy, and attention as you engage in the day's activities. Are you spending your time, energy, and attention in ways that help you implement your priorities and important to-do items, or do you get distracted, sabotage yourself with multitasking, or get sucked into a messy work space or social networking black hole? When you experience leaks in your time, energy, and attention, what activity or mode of operating is enabling the leak to take place? Review the leaks defined earlier in the chapter and see if you fall into any of those patterns—or perhaps you recognize a leak in your day that is not listed there.

Specifically, as the week progresses, take time, in your *7 Keys Workbook and Journal* or other work space, to write down and describe all of the leaks in time, energy, and attention that you have noticed in your day. Be as detailed as possible, describing when the leak occurred, what you were doing, how it felt, and the impact. You may record the leak when you notice it, or you may take time each day or every other day to reflect back, define, and record the leaks. Aim to identify five to ten leaks that occur throughout your week.

◆　◆　◆

Once you are aware of your leaks, you can begin to look at ways to remediate them. The following section will provide guidance on that process.

Putting the Key Into Practice

To manage your day more efficiently, there are specific actions you can engage in to stop your leaks. These actions are what I call *plugs*. Plugs are both reactive and proactive. You initially utilize them to stop a leak—and, if you continue to use the plug, it will stop the leak from recurring. Ideally, a new, more efficient behavior pattern will develop and continue.

Plug Your Leaks

To review, some of the leaks you may face in managing your day include . . .

- multitasking
- lack of planning time
- no support structure
- no delegation
- clutter/messy office or work space
- social networking black hole.

The following text describes plugs that you can use to stop these particular leaks.

Time box is a plug for multitasking. To implement this plug, you will set aside time for specific functions in which you just work on a single function: email time, returning phone call time, marketing project time, research time, creative writing time, home project time, and so on—whichever functions are relevant to you. You do this by actually scheduling the specific task that is a priority for you. This means putting an entry in your calendar or PDA that says "Email" from 8–8:30 a.m. This process has many values.

- First, you are committing to doing what you have scheduled. If you elevate the importance of this activity by scheduling it, it is more likely to happen.
- Second, by having a start and end time to the activity, it will not bleed into other parts of your day.
- Third, you will focus on a single function, so you are likely to be more efficient. Remember, people's brains work better when they focus on one activity at a time rather than multitasking.

Being deliberate as to how you use your time will help you accomplish the activities that are most important to you, in the shortest amount of time, while managing your time, energy, and attention effectively.

Planning time is a plug for lack of planning time. Setting aside even five minutes each day for daily planning, or fifteen to twenty minutes for weekly planning, can make a huge impact in your efficiency. You will shift from doing what others want you to do, toward choosing instead what makes the most sense for you to work on, given your priorities and responsibilities. To build planning into your life, you will want to develop a routine that meshes with your personal work style. For example, if you are most alert at the beginning of the day, you might take the first five minutes at your desk each morning to look at what is on your calendar and what tasks are in need of your time, energy, and attention—and then make choices on how you will spend your day. If you prefer an evening routine, before you leave the office, wind down with a five-minute review of things to come tomorrow. One of the critical factors with planning time is getting it to become routine, where it becomes a natural part of your day, just as brushing your teeth is.

Get support is a plug for no support structure. To fill the no-support-structure leak, you need to know who can assist you in being more efficient and ask for that help. Many highly intelligent, highly accomplished professionals miss out on opportunities to make their work (and life) much less complicated and more effective and efficient because they do not seek or build a support structure around themselves. Who around you can help you do more of the things at which you excel? This means surrounding yourself with, or at least being aware of, others who do certain things better than you! Here are just a few ideas on how to draw on a support structure.

- Your administrative assistant can schedule your time, including meetings, phone calls, and even your uninter-ruptible planning time. For many, giving up control of their calendars is initially a challenge. To be most successful here, you will want to develop a system that both meets your needs for some control and frees you up from the no-value-added tasks of scheduling.
- Know what you do not need to know, and then find the person whose job it is to know. In other words, utilize experts. For example, if your job is to write a "white paper" that will eventually go on your company's website, you need to focus on sharing your expertise and writing it down. You do not have to learn HTML coding to format

the paper for the website and you do not need to spend time understanding the technology of distributing the paper. Rely instead on your company's website administrator to tell you what specifications you need to consider. Know when going beyond your area of responsibility is a waste of your time, energy, and attention and even doing someone else's job.

- Think about what kind of technologies you can start utilizing to free up more of your time, energy, and attention. For example, you can sign up for automatic bill payment, you can arrange to have your prescriptions automatically renewed and sent to you when they get close to being done, and you can do your grocery shopping online, without ever leaving your house. Automated services such as these are becoming more and more prevalent, oftentimes at little-to-no charge.

- A neighborhood teenager can assist you with nonwork activities like picking up dry-cleaning, running to the post office, walking your dog, and even grocery shopping. You can also consider hiring a cleaning person or someone to cook meals for you. Look for ways to simplify your nonwork responsibilities so you do not feel like you need to accomplish everything in your limited hours of waking time. Craig's List (www.CraigsList.com) is a great online resource for finding local service providers for just about anything.

Delegation is a plug for no delegation. Delegation involves asking other people to help you because they are more appropriate for the task. It is a process that allows you to focus on what you do best while also allowing others (usually your direct reports; sometimes colleagues and even occasionally your supervisors and others more senior to you) to do the things at which they excel. In the process, delegation gives more opportunities for growth, leadership, and effectiveness for everyone involved. Because no-delegation is a common leak and plugging this leak brings significant value to you and your workplace situation, we will explore techniques for using delegation in more depth later in the chapter.

Organize is a plug for clutter/messy office or work space.
Put aside time to create an environment that is conducive for efficiency—for most people, that means an organized physical space. It also includes an ordered technological space (computer files) and mental space (brain). There are three fundamental steps to organizing your work space.

First, make sure your working environment feels right to you. If working at your office, cubicle, desk, or kitchen table makes you feel depressed, drained, bored, agitated, uncomfortable, pained, or any other obviously negative descriptors, you need to make some immediate changes to improve the environment in your work space. For example, if every time you reach for your files, your back hurts, you need to rearrange or come up with a new filing system that does not cause you pain. If you thrive on sunlight and love the outdoors but your office has no windows, you need to be creative and add touches of nature by bringing in plants and photos that give you some positive feelings. The overall goal in this first step is to make sure your office or work space does not make you feel bad. Then you can focus on knowing where everything is that you need. There is no one right way to organize. Your system just needs to work for you so you are not spending more time finding what you need than working on what you choose.

If you cannot do this type of organizational work on your own, get the assistance of a more organized friend or colleague, or hire a recommended professional organizer. One warning (or caveat) about organizing—do not let the process of organizing get in the way of doing what is important. Many people use the need for an organized desk as a roadblock to start important work. Sometimes it feels easier to organize than to tackle a challenge. If you need to put time aside for organizing, plan for it. Schedule ten minutes each day or thirty minutes each week for a space cleanup. For resources that can assist you with organization, see the *List of Resources for Learning More* in the Appendix.

Second, you will want to make sure you know where everything is on your computer. When you need to review an article that a colleague has sent you, do you spend twenty minutes searching through 300 emails in your inbox? Or do you have a "professional literature" folder on your hard drive? Develop systems that enable you to find what you need quickly on the computer, whether a message in your email, a file on your hard drive, or a frequently used website online.

Third, how much "clutter" is in your brain? If you are processing too many thoughts or ideas at once, you are likely to feel overwhelmed and unfocused. As David Allen writes in his book, *Getting Things Done*, he likens a cluttered brain to a computer's overloaded RAM—if there are too many programs opened at once, the computer will be very slow and will possibly crash. His system encourages working on one project and only one task at a time, and always knowing what is next and how to find it.

These are just a few plugs that can be used to fix leaks. To learn more about how to plug leaks, let's look at how Grace, mentioned earlier, plugged her particular leak. When identifying her leak, Grace wrote the following.

> *Throughout the day, I constantly check my email when I hear it entering my mailbox, specifically to respond to messages from Joel and Suzanne, my two Senior Project Managers. I want to be able to respond to them right away, no matter what.*

After contemplating the right plug for this leak, Grace wrote the following.

> *Tell Joel and Suzanne, along with the rest of my staff, that email is not the best way to communicate with me if they need an immediate answer. Let them know that I'll be checking my email at the beginning of my work day, before lunch, and at the end of the day. If they need information or input from me outside of this time frame, my cell phone is the way to reach me for urgent, time-sensitive issues.*

Although Grace may still receive interruptions in the form of phone calls from time to time, her project managers are likely to think twice before picking up the phone as Grace has explained that the phone is for urgent, time-sensitive issues. In addition, phone is often a quicker way to resolve issues than by email, so Grace may save some time here, too. Furthermore, Grace will know it is okay to leave her email for checking only during certain planned times of the day. That is, she will be able to focus better on her priority tasks as she sits at her desk since she will no longer be distracted by the feeling that she has to check email for urgent messages.

Now it is time for you to personalize these ideas to plug your own leaks.

Design Your Own Plugs: You have defined your leaks and you are aware of a few possible plugs. When you are ready, revisit the leaks you identified earlier in the chapter (*Identify Your Leaks* fieldwork) and prepare to get specific on how you can remedy them. For each leak you identified, try to come up with small actions that you can do to lessen or stop the specific inefficiency or energy drain. Be creative ... there is no one right answer ... just what works for you in changing behaviors that do not serve you.

As you design plugs to fill your leaks in time, energy, and attention, consider the following key points.

- Think about the possible plugs for your leaks when you are removed from the actual situation. Instead of spending time during your day trying to fix your leaks (thus creating another leak!), you will want to take time outside of the work environment to creatively brainstorm possible plugs.

- When brainstorming on plugs for your leaks, remember that anything is possible. You may have more than one plug for a specific leak. There may be multiple steps that need to be implemented for a specific plug. The point of this exercise is to get you thinking about and feeling that you can create alternate ways of operating that enhance your efficiency and energy. Put your problem-solving hat on and try to have some fun with this process.

- The exercise of designing your plugs is not about implementing. This is a thinking and planning exercise. You will put them into action later.

When you are ready, take out your *7 Keys Workbook and Journal* or other dedicated work space and write down a list of plugs for the corresponding leaks you identified earlier in the chapter. This process will help you lay a foundation for greater efficiency in your day.

Delegation Is a Plug for No Delegation: A Special Leak/Plug to Address

When reviewing the leaks and plugs identified in the earlier fieldwork exercises in this chapter (the *Identify Your Leaks* fieldwork as well as the *Design Your Own Plugs* fieldwork), most likely a lack of delegation or a strong need for delegation will be present. The task of delegation is consistently one of the biggest challenges people have in the workplace and at home. Most people are aware of the importance of effective delegation, but nonetheless they do not use delegation when it would serve them. Because of this, a special section and hands-on exercise related to delegation follows.

Delegation is an integral part of managing your day efficiently. The problem people often have with delegation is related to false messages that they often tell themselves about the delegation process. Some of these messages include the following:

- "How can I ask someone else to do something if it's my job? I don't want to impose."
- "If I ask someone else to do something, then it will show that I'm not capable."
- "If someone else can do what I'm supposed to do, it means I might be replaceable."
- "I should be able to do it all."

If delegation is a challenge for you, you most likely have misconceptions about the intention, process, and/or benefits of this important process. Take a few minutes now to determine what might be getting in the way of more effective delegation for you. If it is helpful, bring out your *7 Keys Workbook and Journal* or turn to your other dedicated work space and write down your thoughts on the kinds of things getting in the way of your effective delegation.

When you are ready, consider a new approach to delegation. Delegation is …

- required if you want to be at your most effective and efficient
- required if you want to develop other leaders within your organization
- desired by your direct reports so they can have opportunities for growth and skill enhancement
- expected of you so you are focusing on your highest value-producing contributions.

So, how do you go about actually delegating responsibilities to others? Once you get comfortable that delegation is a win–win situation for everyone involved, the act becomes much easier. It can be as simple as these few words.

- "Olivia, I have a project that I need assistance on. Can you please do *x*, *y*, and *z* and get it back to me by tomorrow at 2:00 p.m.?"
- "Adam, since you're an expert on _____, can you please write me three paragraphs about that process and send me a draft on Friday?
- "Melissa, can you do *a*, *b*, and *c* for me before the end of the week and let me know when it's completed. This will give you a chance to contribute significantly to the Horton Project. Thank you."

Thus, there are only a few things you need to keep in mind when using delegation:

- find the best person for the job
- ask directly and concisely for what you need
- be specific about time requirements and deadlines
- be respectful and appreciative.

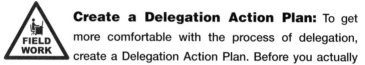 **Create a Delegation Action Plan:** To get more comfortable with the process of delegation, create a Delegation Action Plan. Before you actually attempt to use delegation, complete the following steps: (a) define the task you want to delegate and (b) identify the person to whom you want to delegate the task. You will also want to consider: What does successful completion of this task look like? Be as specific as possible when answering that question. Also, when do you need the project completed and returned to you?

Once you have defined specific needs and requirements for this delegation, spend a few minutes imagining yourself speaking with the person to whom you plan to delegate this work. Write down a possible script for you to use when asking for delegation assistance. Be sure to be direct, concise, respectful, and appreciative.

Here are a few final things to consider regarding delegation.

- What can get in the way of you actually delegating the given task?

- How can you overcome this possible roadblock to delegation?

- What will be the benefit of actually using delegation? (Consider the benefits to you, to the person with whom you are delegating, and to the organization.)

Lastly, make a commitment to using delegation by completing the following statement here or in your *7 Keys Workbook and Journal* or other dedicated work space:

*I will ask _____ to do _____ for me
and complete and return it to my by _____.*

◆　◆　◆

You have now defined one act of delegation to plug a time or energy leak and have committed to the process. It is likely that there are many more opportunities for you to benefit from delegation, but this will be a great place to start.

As you delegate more frequently, the process will become easier and more natural. You will also see your productivity increase and your hesitation with delegation diminish.

Implement Your Plugs

You have defined your leaks and created your plugs, including a plug for the no-delegation leak, if relevant. Now you are ready to choose one specific plug that you would like to implement and then to reflect on the positive result that occurs from using that plug—but, first, let's return to the example of Grace, to see the positive results she encountered after implementing her first plug. To review, Grace's plug was as follows.

My first plug to implement is: Tell Joel and Suzanne, along with the rest of my staff, that email is not the best way to communicate with me if they need an immediate answer. Let them know that I'll be checking my email at the beginning of my workday, before lunch and at the end of the day. If they need information or input from me outside of this time frame, my cell phone is the way to reach me for urgent, time-sensitive issues.

After implementing this plug, Grace described the following positive result.

Joel and Suzanne had no problem with me telling them not to email for important issues. It was completely a nonissue. They said they're fine calling me when they need urgent responses. Suzanne even seemed relieved as she didn't like waiting and not knowing when I'd get back to her. This gave her more immediate access to me when she really needed it and made me feel more comfortable not checking my email 200 times a day. What a relief!

 Plug Your Leaks: Now, it is your turn. Select the first plug that you will put into action. Be as detailed as possible, describing what you will do. Write the plug somewhere visible so you will see it each day, and start your day reminding yourself what new action you will take to enhance your time, energy, and attention management. After you implement your first plug, record in your *7 Keys Workbook and Journal* (or other dedicated work space) a positive result from making this change.

As you begin to implement your first plug, pay attention to how you feel when you try out the new behavior. If it feels right, meaning that it fits with your style and it is giving you the results that you want, keep doing it. If it does not feel right, or if it is not producing the desired results, change it. Regardless of what change you are making, it is critical that the change fit with your personal style and preferences, or you are very likely not to continue it.

After you feel comfortable with the first plug you implemented, choose another. Each time, give yourself time and space to get used to the new behavior change and to observe the results. Eventually, each plug will become a new and more effective and efficient way of operating.

Be sure to share the plugs that you are implementing with those with whom you interact so they are aware of the changes you are making and will understand your new way of operating. You can also seek others' assistance in supporting your new behavior. Ideally, using the plug will create a win–win situation for everyone involved. You will be more efficient and productive and you will be role-modeling behavior that can enhance others' efficiency and productivity.

- A leak is an action or lack-of-action that increases demands on your time, energy, or attention.
- Pay attention/look for leaks—either old ones returning or new ones you are just noticing. Make this part of a regular efficiency evaluation process.
- Some common leaks include multitasking, no planning time, no support structure, no delegation, clutter/messy office or work space, and social networking black hole.
- Once you have identified a leak, allow time to define an appropriate plug.
- Delegation is a critical and learnable skill for increasing efficiency.
- Implement one plug and observe results. Continue this process with a pattern of implementation and observation.
- Continue to monitor improved results, and always make adjustments as needed.

KEY 4

Design Reasonable Expectations

As you are making your way through this book and focusing on improving your work–life balance, you are likely bringing many expectations to the process. Perhaps you expect that by the time you finish reading this book, you will have made some small adjustments to your professional life that will help you enjoy your personal life more. Perhaps, instead, you anticipate much more sweeping change—for example, that by book's end, you will have really perfected your whole work–life balance "project," such that you will have figured out how to "have it all" without giving anything up.

Expectations are important in that they can set us up for success. The expectation that we are going to accomplish something can provide us with a clear target to aim for and can ultimately increase the likelihood that our expectation will be accomplished and met.

Yet, expectations can also set us up for failure if they are unreasonable. Sometimes we expect things of ourselves that cannot be realistically accomplished. As a result, we end up failing to meet that particular expectation and/or undermining our own abilities to accomplish everything else on our list of to-do's, responsibilities, and priorities.

For example, if someone reads this book and expects to have achieved perfect work–life balance by the time the book is over, those expectations are unlikely to be met and thus are unreasonable. Disappointment and frustration will probably follow. Similarly, if a person expects to read this book within a short time frame, this is also an unreasonable expectation. He might be able to get to the last page within a few days, but will he be able to do all of the exercises? Probably not. If he does do all the exercises, what else in his life will he have to give up to do so?

People who struggle to bring more work–life balance into their world sometimes have difficulty setting reasonable expectations for themselves. Instead of seeing the limits of what is humanly possible for themselves—given their time availability, finite energy resources, and current responsibilities—they often overestimate their own capacity to deliver output for themselves and others. As a consequence, they end up running themselves ragged by trying to accomplish the impossible and move further away from their desired balance.

This chapter will help you identify whether reasonable expectations is one of the missing keys to your work–life balance. If you discover that it is, you will have an opportunity to identify and examine your (and other people's) unreasonable expectations of you and then to alter these expectations in a way that moves you closer to your ideal work–life balance and away from the tiring hamster wheel that has you feeling like you are running without ever getting anywhere.

Developing Awareness of the Key

A Closer Look at the Concept

An *expectation* refers to something that is desired for the future. The expectations you have of yourself represent what you would like to do in the future or how you would like to be in the future. Expectations that others have of you represent what others would like you to do or how others would like you to be in the future.

Expectations have many benefits, such as helping you achieve at a high level. In particular, expectations are useful because when you have clearly defined the future you want for yourself, these expectations give you a place to focus your efforts. For example, during the past two years, I had an expectation to complete my manuscript and publish this book. During this time, this expectation helped me focus a significant amount of my time and energy working on this project. Expectations also provide you with a benchmark to evaluate your progress and then determine whether you need to implement any behavior changes to better support you in achieving what you want. In the case of the previous example, this might mean evaluating my progress regularly on my book completion to see if I have fulfilled or am close to fulfilling my desired expectation.

Thus, the expectations we have for ourselves can remind us of what is important, by acting as a road map of what we want to accomplish.

Now let's consider the expectations that others have of us, as well as those we have of others. Let's begin with others' expectations. Others' expectations of us let us know what matters to others and how we fit into the bigger picture of the groups of which we are a part—family, employer, community, and others. For example, if my boss let's me know that as HR director I am responsible for attending all company social functions because this sets a good example for staff and gives employees easy access to me, I will know that it is important to my boss (and perhaps my job) that I make attending company social functions a priority. (If I disagree or this is problematic for me, I can have a conversation with my boss to adjust expectations in a way that works for all of us—the organization, my boss, and myself).

In turn, having expectations of others and expressing them allows others to understand how you will act and interact with them. For example, Gretchen is a magazine editor and it is her expectation that her boss will not give her unnecessary work to do during the three days that lead up to the monthly deadline for sending the magazine to print because she is incredibly busy during this time with essential, deadline-related tasks. Once she has communicated these expectations to her boss, she and her boss will have a mutual understanding of what her core responsibilities are in the three days leading up to the magazine deadline and what she needs from her boss in order to do her job well.

The challenge arises when expectations become unreasonable. This typically occurs when we use words like "must," "should," or "always" or when we set unmanageable time frames to accomplish certain tasks. In these cases, expectations become a ticking time bomb or a treadmill that cannot be stopped. These unreasonable expectations, which either we have or others have of us, sabotage our work–life balance. As we are unlikely to ever meet these expectations, they are simply setting us up for eventual disappointment and frustration.

In addition, the energy we spend trying to meet these unreasonable expectations might ultimately go to waste, as the opportunity to meet these expectations expires.

By setting unreasonable expectations for yourself, you may simply be increasing your workload and undermining your other important priorities and responsibilities, without any real promise of achieving your desired result. If you do achieve the desired result, you may still end up feeling discouraged, demotivated, or dissatisfied because of the cost you paid in the process of meeting your unreasonable expectations. Here is an example.

> Bill, a young financial analyst, was starting out in a new position in a very demanding and stressful environment. He always took on requests from his more senior colleagues, often working eighty-hour weeks if needed. Instead of being rewarded with a quicker promotion as he hoped, though, he was simply labeled "the worker bee" and was given lots of work that no one else wanted to do. He was able to accomplish a lot, but it was not the quality of work he wanted to be doing nor was it focusing on his professional interests and goals. He was overworked, overwhelmed, and dissatisfied with the direction of his career path.

What backfired for Bill in this case? Both his unreasonable expectations of himself ("I should do everything that anyone asks me to do as it will make me look good and I will be seen as a competent and capable team player") and unreasonable expectations that others had of him ("The new young guy has lots of energy and time and seems very eager, so I'll give him all of the grunt work. He can do it.") Both of these expectations working together trapped Bill in a role without much opportunity for more interesting and challenging work or for being seen as a future leader.

What Is Unreasonable?

Although the answer to this question is very subjective, unreasonable expectations are generally those that . . .

- cause you to make excuses
- cause you to feel guilty
- cause you to feel resentful
- cause you to feel incompetent or incapable.

This list is not meant to be exhaustive but to provide you with a starting point for thinking about where in your own life you might be experiencing unreasonable expectations. Do any of these situations sound familiar? Perhaps you would add other items to this list as you reflect on the toll that unreasonable expectations are having on your own life.

Now let's look at another example of someone who sets unreasonable expectations for himself and has moved away from work–life balance as a result.

Matthew is a web designer and graphic artist with his own company. Over the past four years, he has developed a very successful business in his regional market by staying readily available to answer all of his clients' demands and by meeting or often beating their tight deadlines. His obsession with fantastic customer service has served him well. Most of his business is now coming from returning clients and referrals so that he is spending less time on marketing and business development and more time on his favorite element of the business, project work. Nonetheless, Matthew is running out of steam because in his efforts to make clients happy, he sets unreasonable expectations for himself that lead him to work until 3:00 or 4:00 a.m. a few nights each week while still maintaining early morning appointments with current and potential clients. Not only is his lack of sleep leaving Matthew feeling exhausted, but he also misses time with his girlfriend, his guitar, and his workout regimen.

A major reason that work–life balance eludes Matthew is because he sets unreasonable expectations for himself at work. For example, he expects himself to deliver perfect customer service (i.e., being available twenty-four hours a day), he expects himself to perform well with minimal sleep, and he expects himself to deliver work within an unrealistic time frame. In short, he is expecting more of himself than is humanly possible if he hopes to end his workday at a reasonable hour and have some time left over for his personal priorities and to-do items.

Understandably, there may be many times that Matthew has to work beyond an eight-hour workday, given the deadline-oriented nature of his business, but he might also be able to gain more time most days after work by designing project timelines based on more reasonable expectations of himself and his potential output. If Matthew desires enhanced work–life balance, he will need to spend some time adjusting his own (and likely others') expectations to be more reasonable.

What Is Reasonable?

As with unreasonable expectations, the meaning of reasonable expectations is also completely subjective. What is reasonable to you may be completely unreasonable to your friend, partner, boss, or child—and, vice versa. As a result, setting reasonable expectations can be challenging. Even so, I encourage you to choose what feels fair, achievable, manageable, and motivating to *you*. In a world where your work and life feel more balanced, you get to decide which expectations fit with your work, your personality, your preferences, and your values. Once you have set your personal version of reasonable expectations, you can *then* moderate it within the context of other people's needs.

Note that I referred to other people's "needs" in that previous sentence, not their "expectations." This is because what people *need* and what they *expect* is not always the same thing. For example, Matthew's clients might expect him to return a new logo mock–up to them within 48 hours because that is how fast he normally works, but they might not really need the logo until a meeting that is taking place a week from now. If Matthew allows himself to set expectations that fit with his preferences first, and then runs his desired timeline by his client, he might discover that with some negotiation, he can create a timeline that leaves everyone happy. In sum, Matthew cannot control his clients' perceptions, but he can bring his and their expectations to light and try to negotiate for a situation that is *reasonable* for both of them while increasing his own work–life balance satisfaction.

Identifying the Barrier: Unreasonable Expectations

As has been discussed thus far in the chapter, the challenge that unreasonable expectations can cause to work–life balance originates in two different sources—*others'* unreasonable expectations of you as well as *your own* unreasonable expectations of yourself. As you try to assess whether you face the barrier of *unreasonable expectations* on your path to enhanced work–life balance, consider the expectations that others have for you as well as the expectations that you create for yourself.

Others' Unreasonable Expectations of Us

As mentioned earlier, the nature of "unreasonable" is a subjective thing. As a result, I am not expecting you to determine in any objective way whether someone else's expectations are unreasonable so much as I am encouraging you to tune into whether these expectations feel unreasonable to you.

There are multiple reasons that may cause us to feel that others' expectations of us are unreasonable. Because these expectations involve another person, one factor of "unreasonableness" may be that both parties do not share the same expectation or it is not clearly defined or communicated. For example, a colleague comes to your office and asks you to proofread a document for him. He leaves it on your desk. He stops by your office the next day and is noticeably upset and frustrated at you, and then asks where his document is. It is still in your inbox where he left it. You apologize and also feel a bit annoyed. You were working on a big project and he did not ask you to review the document within a specific time frame. His unreasonable expectation of you was that you would take care of his request right away. You did not share the same expectation nor did he communicate his expectation to you. As is clear in this example, lack of communication between two people can lead to the feeling that an expectation is unreasonable.

You may also see an expectation as unfair, unachievable, or inappropriate. For example, because you are consistently the best salesperson on your sales team, your boss has given you a sales goal, without any additional support, for the upcoming year that is 30% higher than all of your colleagues. She sees this as a way of acknowledging and encouraging you; you see it as almost impossible and that it will prevent you from ever having an evening off from work.

Examples of unreasonable expectations that others may have of you include the following. (Note that these quotes represent someone else's perspective or thoughts about you.)

- "She can solve any problem ... I always go to her!"
- "He's so organized; of course he can handle another small project."
- "She doesn't have kids so it won't be a problem if I ask her to work late."
- "He's so approachable, he won't mind if I knock on his door."
- "We don't need outside help around the house ... my wife (or husband or partner) manages work, the kids, and the house just fine."
- "She will always drop everything for my needs ... that's what sisters (or daughters or mothers) do!"
- "He's a tech whiz ... of course he'll help me fix my computer."

Later in the chapter, I will invite you to spend some time looking at how you can work with others in a shared process of negotiating reasonable expectations of you. Before you begin that process, though, it will be helpful first to observe where these unreasonable expectations are currently happening in your professional and personal life.

As a review, unreasonable expectations are those that cause you to make excuses, cause you to feel guilty, cause you to feel resentful, or cause you to feel incompetent or incapable.

 Identify the Unreasonable Expectations of Others: Over the next week, pay attention to interactions you have with others and identify where unreasonable expectations may be impacting your desired work–life balance. After you have identified these unreasonable expectations, for each one describe the impact of the unreasonable expectation and a factor that you believe may be causing the unreasonable expectation. Write this information in your *7 Keys Workbook and Journal* or other dedicated work space. For example, you might start by writing the following.

Unreasonable expectation: My boss continues to expect me to meet forty-five billable hours each week, even though I've been given additional administrative responsibility.

Next, you would want to write down the impact you believe this unreasonable expectation is having on your work, life, and/or work–life balance.

Impact: I am focusing more on quantity than quality of my work. As a result, the quality of my work is suffering and I am feeling overwhelmed at work. I am also staying later at the office than I used to, which causes me to miss my nightly jog.

Lastly, you would want to try to identify whichever factor (or factors) you believe is causing the unreasonable expectation (so you can eventually develop a plan to alter this expectation). Toward that effort, you might write the following.

Cause: I did not inform my boss that I had taken on additional administrative responsibility to support another manager, nor did I redefine billable hours expectations with my boss after taking on this additional responsibility.

As you work through this process, give yourself freedom to write down each and every expectation of you by others that you feel is unreasonable and that is having a negative impact on your work or personal life. Later, when creating a plan to alter these unreasonable expectations, you can moderate these against the reality of life or any constraints that you face in making adjustments. You might even reflect and decide that an expectation is not as unreasonable as you first thought. For now, though, allow yourself the freedom to write down all of your thoughts related to unreasonable expectations. Later, you can pull back if needed.

◆　◆　◆

Now that you have identified other people's unreasonable expectations of you, it is time to take a look at the unreasonable expectations you have of yourself.

Unreasonable Expectations of Yourself

When it comes to unreasonable expectations, the even more challenging situation is changing expectations you have for *yourself*. This requires you to change thoughts and behaviors that you have likely had for a long period of time and that you may believe are extremely beneficial to you. To move closer toward your ideal work–life balance, though, you will need to develop more reasonable expectations of yourself—kinder and gentler expectations that still allow you to accomplish at the level you wish without taking on more responsibility than is needed or beneficial (i.e., without compromising your desired work–life balance).

Your own unreasonable expectations often go unnoticed because they may be supported by behaviors that make you extremely effective, efficient, and productive and that ultimately get you recognized in a very positive way, both professionally and personally. Perhaps this reality might cause you to feel reluctant to adjust your unreasonable expectations. Yet, having high standards, achieving outstanding results, and accomplishing more and better does not have to happen at the expense of your desired work–life balance. As mentioned earlier, it is the unreasonable nature of expectations that have the negative impact, not expectations in general.

When we look at our own expectations, the flag for unreasonableness can be seen in the extreme language we use to describe our desired results. For example, consider the following extreme language.

- "I should be able to do everything myself."
- "I always need to be available—clients are paying a lot of money for my services."
- "This is just the way it is for a banker, lawyer, doctor, actor, management consultant [fill-in-the-blank]. I just need to grin and bear it."
- "No one else can do the work as well as I can."
- "I can't say no to anyone in my family."
- "I should be able to keep my house in order."
- "I need to respond to my colleagues in less than an hour."
- "I always can find some time for important causes."

Perhaps some of these statements are sounding familiar to you, or maybe you are even thinking of other thoughts that sometimes run through your head and that set up unreasonable expectations for yourself.

Later, I will invite you to redefine your own expectations at a more reasonable level, but, first, I am going to ask you to identify how your own unreasonable expectations are currently showing up in your day-to-day actions and beliefs, along with the negative impact that they are having on your work–life balance.

Identify Your Unreasonable Expectations of Yourself: Over the next week, pay attention to your thoughts, choices, and behaviors as you go about engaging in your personal and professional responsibilities. Observe when you think or use extreme words such as "I must," "I should," or "I always." These are often signs of unreasonable expectations. After you have identified the unreasonable expectation, describe, in your *7 Keys Workbook and Journal* or other dedicated work space, the impact of the unreasonable expectation on your current work–life balance situation.

For example, you might start by identifying the following unreasonable expectation that you have of yourself.

> *My unreasonable expectation: I shouldn't leave the office without following up on all of my staff's requests from the day.*

This unreasonable expectation is likely to have continual consequences in your life, but for this exercise, try to think of one specific time that it has recently impacted you. Then write about it. For example, you might write the following.

> *Impact: On Wednesday I cancelled my 7:00 p.m. personal trainer appointment at the gym so I could work another few hours and deal with all of my staff's requests that day. By the time I left, though, I still hadn't filled all of the requests. As a result, I left the office feeling dissatisfied, like I didn't do enough. And, I missed my gym appointment, which lessened my energy for the week and made me feel bad about two things instead of just one.*

As you can see with this example, a single unreasonable expectation can have multiple consequences. Just imagine what would happen if you looked at how this unreasonable expectation affected you over a period of days or weeks. The consequences would multiply even further.

Take some time now to write down your list of unreasonable expectations. Next, describe the impact of each of those unreasonable expectations on your current work–life balance situation.

◆ ◆ ◆

Before you go on to the next section, take a breath. You have just made significant progress on your journey toward work–life balance by identifying your own and other people's unreasonable expectations of you. As the old saying goes, knowledge is power, and now you have some valuable knowledge and personal insight that you can use to formulate a plan for adjusting your own and others' expectations so they support you in moving toward your desired work–life balance.

Putting the Key Into Practice

Awareness is a very important part of the process of improving your work–life balance, but you also need to be able to act on that awareness—to make changes in yourself and the world around you. This section of the chapter will give you some useful tools for making the changes necessary to reframe your own and others' expectations so they are more reasonable.

Negotiating Expectations With Others

Now that you are aware of the unreasonable expectations others may have of you and how these expectations are impacting you, you can work to negotiate a change regarding these unreasonable expectations. This next step requires communication—letting the other party know your reality, that is, what you see as the specific issue or concern related to the unreasonable expectation. As this expectation is discussed between you and someone else, you will then need to redefine a more mutually agreeable expectation.

Communicating your concerns. To begin the dialogue, you will want to communicate in a nondefensive manner in order to be heard and get results. You can achieve this manner by starting the conversation with an "I" statement, which means you will point out how the unreasonable expectation impacts you. An "I statement" is when you share your feelings, concerns, or perspective with someone by beginning the sentence with "I." This allows you to take ownership of what is happening to you without blaming the situation on the person with whom you are speaking.

When stating your concern in a nondefensive manner, you use language that does not pass blame or judgment about the other person. You let the person know how something affects you and how you feel about it. (You will also state what you need instead, as described in the next section). This enables the person to whom you are speaking to actually hear what you are saying and, hopefully, to respond in a supportive way.

For example, when using an "I" statement with her supervisor, tax accountant, Lauren, might say the following.

> Patty, I notice that you often give me important projects just as I'm leaving for the day. Unfortunately, this often causes me to leave later from work than I had planned, which requires me to cancel previously scheduled personal commitments.

We can infer from the previous statement that Patty's unreasonable expectation is the following: Lauren is available at any time of day to take on new projects and that her schedule is very flexible for meeting Patty's needs. Yet, note that instead of describing the unreasonable expectation itself, Lauren does something more effective. She highlights the objective behavior that occurs as a result of this unreasonable expectation ("you often give me important projects as I'm leaving") so that she does her best not to put Patty on the defensive. Next, Lauren explains the effect that this behavior has on her ("this often causes me to leave later from work"). In short, Lauren uses "I" statements to explain the impact of Patty's unreasonable behaviors on Lauren's work and life.

Those of you who are reading the book from start to finish might notice that this example overlaps an example discussed in the chapter on boundaries. This is because unreasonable expectations and boundaries are often related. In this case, Patty has unreasonable *expectations* of Lauren, and Lauren will need to set a *boundary* in the process of realigning expectations. This boundary will relate to Lauren's need to leave work no later than a certain time each day and will be discussed in the following section.

Redefining expectations. The next step in negotiating expectations with others is to collaborate with the other person to redefine a more reasonable expectation. You can do this by clearly stating the more appropriate and reasonable expectation that you want to work and live by as a starting point for your discussion. For example, Lauren might add to her previous statements the following.

As I need to leave by 6:00 p.m., I would appreciate you giving me the work earlier in the day and if you can't do that I will plan to address the work the following morning. How would this work for you?

By sharing with Patty the more reasonable expectation that she not give Lauren work that causes her to leave after 6:00 p.m. (that her professional availability is not unlimited and at Patty's whim but is contained in a specific and very appropriate time frame), but also inviting her to participate in the dialogue, Lauren begins to move toward creating a solution while engaging Patty as a partner in problem solving. Ideally, Patty then becomes a partner in designing a shared, reasonable expectation. The conversation that develops may include negotiation, clarification, and eventually a resolution that works for both parties involved.

In the case of Patty, she might respond by thanking Lauren for letting her know about her personal situation, acknowledging that Lauren's needs are indeed reasonable, and also stressing her own needs and concerns of making sure all projects are done in a time frame that is helpful to Patty. They both agree to continue paying attention to this situation, making sure that all work is completed and giving Lauren more notice and flexibility in completing required work.

Of course, situations do not always work out this neatly, but, often, raising issues like these can be much less scary or frightening than imagined. If Lauren's boss was not so open, for example, a new choice for how to deal with the unreasonable expectation would be put back on Lauren. In particular, Lauren would need to decide whether she can make the current situation work or whether she should try to negotiate something else. (Note that if Lauren's boss was unwilling to negotiate more reasonable expectations, this could be a sign of unbalanced organizational culture, which is covered in its own chapter, later in the book.)

Now that you have seen an example of working with others to reframe their expectations, you are ready to make a plan for giving the process a try yourself. In the following exercise, you will work to reframe someone else's unreasonable expectation of you into a *shared reasonable expectation*.

 Address Others' Unreasonable Expectations: Revisit the list of unreasonable expectations that others have of you that you made earlier in the chapter (see the *Identify the Unreasonable Expectations of Others* fieldwork). Then choose one of the expectations that someone else has of you that you wish to reframe. With this expectation in mind, answer the following questions in your *7 Keys Workbook and Journal* or other dedicated work space.

- What is the unreasonable expectation held of me that I would like to change and who holds it?
- What exactly makes this expectation unreasonable to me?
- What might be a more reasonable expectation that I could propose?
- How do I want to start this conversation? (Remember—use an "I" statement.)
- What reasons can I give to advocate for the new, shared, reasonable expectation?
- What would be the ideal result from this conversation?
- How would my life change if we created a new, shared, reasonable expectation?

As you complete the previous questions, remember that the process in which you are about to engage is dependent on someone else. So, this conversation may not follow a specific road map. Be open to listening to the other person's perspective while sharing your needs and wants for redefining the expectation at hand. During the next week, choose a time to speak with the person you identified with the intention of creating a new, reasonable, and shared expectation.

For some, this process may feel like a very challenging, uncomfortable, or difficult conversation to initiate. If you are not used to asserting your preferences or requesting something from someone else, this process may even feel overwhelming. Before you begin the discussion, remind yourself that this process is about creating a better situation for everyone involved. Also remember that if you are more comfortable with what is expected of you, you will be more effective, happy, efficient, and engaged in your work and in your nonwork activities. In addition, this will have a positive impact on all that you do, personally and professionally, thus creating a win–win situation.

Once you feel some impact from this change, you can revisit the additional unreasonable expectations from others that you identified earlier in the chapter (again, see the *Identify the Unreasonable Expectations of Others* fieldwork) and repeat the process.

Hopefully, the energy you gained from your first expectations adjustment will fuel your desire to continue changing expectations that are no longer working for you. Remember that this is a process. Old unreasonable expectations may disappear and new ones may develop. To stay on top of this, create a regular system for evaluating mutually held expectations and look to address ones that do not serve you.

Reframing Your Own Expectations

Changing your own expectations does not involve collaboration or communication with others. Most often, a shift in perspective is all that is required. Instead of assuming "I always," "I should," or "I must" [fill-in-the-blank], I encourage you to adopt a more reasonable approach that allows for choice, perspective, and individual evaluation of each situation. For example, you might move from the perspective of . . .

> *I must be at every one of my son's school events.*

to a more reasonable . . .

> *I will get to as many of my son's school events as I can and will make arrangements for my husband or mother to get to the rest, as I like someone to be present from the family. It doesn't always have to be me.*

For people who are used to constantly taking on more and more responsibility, doing more and more, and never saying "no" or "not now," defining something reasonable may feel very uncomfortable, like slacking or doing less than is appropriate. If this is a relevant issue for you, try to remember that this process of reframing your expectations is not about trying to get away with doing less. Instead, it is about having confidence that you will never do less than a good job and that you can still do a very good job by setting more reasonable expectations for yourself.

For example, in the earlier case of Lauren, if she begins to decline last-minute work from Patty so she can leave the office as planned, she will have more time in the evenings with her children as well as get to bed a little earlier, which will help her return to work the next day feeling more refreshed and clearheaded. As a result, her productivity at work will remain high and maybe even increase.

 Reframe Your Own Unreasonable Expectations: Now let's begin the process of reframing your own unreasonable expectations by returning in your *7 Keys Workbook and Journal* or other dedicated work space to the list you created earlier in the chapter of your own unreasonable expectations (see the *Identify Your Unreasonable Expectations of Yourself* fieldwork). Once you have this list handy, take some time to reframe the expectations on this list in a more reasonable fashion. As an example of how to undertake this process, let's return to the unreasonable expectation cited earlier (repeated in the text that follows).

My unreasonable expectation: I shouldn't leave the office without following up on all of my staff's requests from the day.

In this case, you might reframe this unreasonable expectation in the following way.

More reasonable reframe: Since working late doesn't guarantee that I'll get through all the follow-up to staff requests, I can leave after a full day of work and take care of myself. I will then be more energized to tackle any remaining and new staff needs the next day.

Now that you have seen an example of this exercise in practice, turn to your *7 Keys Workbook and Journal* or other dedicated work space and reframe your unreasonable expectations. Once you have written down these new, more reasonable expectations, contemplate how and when you will begin to implement them. Imagine yourself making a mental shift to *thinking* in terms of your new reasonable expectations. Consider as well how your *behaviors* might change as a result of your new, more reasonable expectations (e.g., leave work at 6:00 p.m.

most nights instead of 7:00 p.m.). Since the reframed expectations you define are internally based and do not involve others, you can begin to integrate one, some, or all as soon as you are ready.

◆　◆　◆

Since the process of reframing your expectations requires a mental shift, you will likely need to revisit and remind yourself of the change in perspective often. Try to remember that this process will not work as an overnight fix. Changing perspective on anything requires time to allow the new way of thinking to become more natural and for its benefits to be felt.

Underpromise and Overdeliver: A Strategy to Set Reasonable Expectations in Advance

Consider the strategy of "underpromise and overdeliver," which means promising less, and delivering sooner, or better, than you stated.

By promising just a little bit less to others, you will still be accomplishing at or above most people's reasonable expectations. For example, instead of telling a colleague that you can get him a rough draft of an article in a week (which you know is the shortest possible time frame you can manage), let him know it will be two weeks. If he needs it sooner, he will let you know. If he does not, you just bought yourself an extra week and some breathing room. Now, if you get it done sooner, you are a star; you *overdelivered*— and you scheduled it on your terms without making yourself crazy.

You can also use this concept for shorter time increments. If your normal response to your boss is to drop everything when she asks you to do something, experiment by responding to a request with a more reasonable time frame. Try saying, "I'll get to that in two hours" instead of "I'll get it for you right away." Those two hours will give you time to decide how to best approach the request and to redesign your schedule for that day. The extra time will allow you to consider your other responsibilities and how they all fit together in accomplishing your overall plan for the day. Again, if your boss needs the work immediately, she would tell you. This process gives you the opportunity to make choices in how you manage your time, your projects, and yourself, which ultimately affects your satisfaction with your work–life balance.

How do you want to experiment with "underpromise and overdeliver?" Over the next two weeks, look for an opportunity to underpromise and overdeliver. When you have a deadline to meet, or someone asks you to do something, add some padding to the time by which you would normally say you would have the task completed. After you have engaged in this exercise, consider your answers to the following questions and write them down in your *7 Keys Workbook and Journal* or other dedicated work space. How did it feel to underpromise? How did it impact the way you accomplished the task? How did it feel when you overdelivered? What direct feedback did you receive regarding the completion of the task?

If you were satisfied with the benefit and results of underpromising and overdelivering, how do you want to further incorporate this strategy into your daily activities? If you were not satisfied with underpromising and overdelivering, how might you tweak that process to work better for you? Alternately, in what other way(s) can you give yourself permission to create more reasonable expectations for yourself?

Changing your expectations of yourself is not an easy task. For many, it is both a difficult and scary process. Difficult because it requires changing patterns that you have had for a long time; scary because you are concerned that you may not provide what you believe others expect of you.

So, as you begin this process, know that this is a *big deal*— and, with that knowledge, be gentle on yourself.

As you create your more reasonable expectations and begin to implement them, remember the following. Take baby steps. In other words, do not set more unreasonable expectations for yourself regarding this process of changing expectations! Even small changes will have an impact.

In addition, pay attention to the benefits you are getting from more reasonable expectations and enjoy them. Hopefully you will experience less stress and pressure as you work and live in accordance with your more reasonable expectations.

Lastly, ask for feedback from those who might be impacted by your change in expectations. It is likely that they will not see any difference in your work or what you produce, except that they may notice a more relaxed and focused person—and you will be on the road to greater work–life balance!

- Expectations are something that is desired in the future. We have expectations of/for ourselves and others have expectations of/for us.
- Expectations are beneficial when they are motivating and reasonable. They become detrimental to work–life balance when they become unreasonable.
- *Unreasonable* is a subjective term. You get to define what is unreasonable for yourself, or you can do so in conjunction with someone else for a shared expectation.
- You need to identify the unreasonable expectations that you possess or that others have of you in order to adjust or negotiate new expectations.
- Shifting others' expectations requires direct communication, possible negotiation, and then creation of a new, shared reasonable expectation.
- Unreasonable expectations of yourself are often identified by the use of extreme language: "I should," "I must," or "I always."
- Changing your own expectations is often more challenging than changing others' expectations of yourself. It requires a shift or reframe in perspective.
- Underpromise and overdeliver is a strategy to set reasonable expectations in advance.
- Changing any expectation is a challenging endeavor. Attempt it slowly, gently, and without setting new unreasonable expectations.

KEY 5

Reprioritize Your Values

This chapter will take you on a journey of examining your values—what they are, which ones are most important to you, how you really define each of your values, and whether the values you are currently acting upon in your day-to-day life move you closer to your desired work–life balance or, instead, serve as a barrier to your desired work–life balance.

By the end of the chapter, in fact, you will have ten of your core values identified and defined. Some time ago, I engaged in this exercise myself and I now carry my core values in my wallet. Every so often, I pull them out and examine them to see how I am integrating these core values in my day-to-day life. Do they still matter to me? Are they still my "top ten"? Are the choices I am making congruent with my values? If I am currently dissatisfied with the state of my work–life balance, I will also ask—do I need to make an adjustment to place a greater emphasis on one of these values and a lesser emphasis on another one of these values?

Having a clear idea of what your values are and which ones are most important to you can be a very useful key to moving toward your desired work–life balance. When you discover that one of your values is making it hard for you to experience your desired state of balance, you can make a deliberate choice about whether to continue honoring that value or, instead, to give it a lesser priority and honor a different value that brings you closer to your ideal work–life balance. This chapter will walk you through several exercises in clarifying your values so you can identify whether this chapter's key is relevant on your own journey toward work–life balance.

Developing Awareness of the Key

A Closer Look at the Concept

A value can be described as . . .

- a belief that is extremely important to you
- a quality that makes you who you are
- a principle that you uphold in how you choose to live your life.

We all have values and we have many values. For example, my values include respect, competence, knowledge, joy, and beauty. My husband's values include financial security, accomplishment, integrity, and honesty. One of my good friend's values include creativity, family, physical fitness, and community involvement.

Some values are more important to us than others—I call these *core values*. In my case, respect, equality, and knowledge are part of my core values.

In addition, the importance of specific values may fluctuate over time, depending on one's current situation. For example, a recent college graduate living in a new city may value fun, friendships, and career success. When he becomes a thirty-something new parent, he may value time with family, flexibility, and health; by the time he becomes an executive near retirement age, his values may include adventure, financial stability, learning, and contribution. As shown by this example, a person's values may shift as life circumstances change.

Our values impact our actions in a variety of ways. For example, if I value recognition and prestige, I may choose to work long hours at a top-tier architectural firm even though it means that I have very little time to spend with friends because I am always working. Alternately, if I value time with friends and recreation and do not place a high value on prestige and recognition, I may choose to leave the top-tier firm after a year and transfer to a lesser known firm that requires me to work fewer hours and allows me more time with friends and my outdoor activities. Ultimately, the values I possess will affect my behaviors and decisions.

Let's look at the values of Janine, a 50-year-old director of marketing at a Fortune 500 company, to learn more about how values can play a role in work–life balance. The following list represents Janine's core values, as defined by her:

- financial security
- contribution
- accomplishment
- health
- time with family and friends.

Now, let's read on to learn more about Janine's particular situation.

Janine, who is very good at her work, feels that she is contributing to her company as well as to the improvement of society, due to the environmentally-sustainable products created by her company. Although this aspect of Janine's work–life situation aligns with her values of accomplishment and contribution, other aspects of Janine's work–life situation *do not* align with her values, in particular, her values of health and time with family and friends. For example, she works twelve- to fourteen-hour days and travels a significant amount each month, which keeps her away from family and friends. In addition, she spends much of her weekends catching up on basic administrative tasks, like replying to emails and returning voicemails, so that she does not seem to have time to exercise or cook healthy meals for the coming work week. As a result, Janine feels as though her work–life situation is completely out of balance. She has thought about leaving her company for a more sane position but knows she will never get the same salary or stock options that she has accrued during her time at this company. Such a change would threaten her current comfortable lifestyle, her ability to retire in a few years, and her ease in paying for her daughter's college—in sum, it would threaten her value of financial security. Janine feels that she cannot keep up this pace much longer, yet she feels trapped in her current career situation because she fears losing her financial security.

What values were driving Janine's choices and actions? In Janine's situation, financial security was overriding some of her other important values. In particular, she was completely disregarding her values of health and time with family and friends, even though she defined these values as important. So, although Janine was engaging in work that supported her value of financial security (as well as of contribution and accomplishment), her work situation did not currently support her values of health and time with family and friends—values reflective of her preferred work–life balance. Essentially, her value of financial security took precedence over—or was incompatible with—her values of health and time with family and friends. As long as this incompatibility existed, Janine would experience a sense of dissatisfaction with her work–life balance.

> It was not until a personal health crisis occurred that Janine became able to re-evaluate her work and life situation in relation to the values that were important to her. In the process, she came to a realization that financial security, although very important, would not matter if she was too ill (or not around) to enjoy it in ten years. In response, she adjusted her actions to make them more compatible with her values of health and time with family and friends—not just financial security. Now that she has given some priority to health and time with family and friends as core values, she has been engaging in a job search with the assistance of headhunters and has lessened her focus on constant work. She is still maintaining her responsibilities but not with the same sense of urgency. She has decided to look for work that is not so all-consuming and is less concerned with how a job change may impact her salary.

For Janine, although work–life balance was desired, this desire was not what was fueling her decisions before her health crisis. Because of her life situation (a child in college, a comfortable lifestyle, looming retirement), her choices were steered only by her value of financial security. Until she made a deliberate choice to reprioritize (or adjust) her values preferences—making impactful changes around her health and time with family and friends—meeting her desires for work–life balance was not possible. Her goal became to find a job that provided adequately for her financial needs but also allowed her to take care of her health and have time for friends and family. In sum, she worked to adjust her values so they became more compatible with her preferred work–life balance.

One of the keys to help you advance on the journey toward work–life balance is to recognize when one (or more) of your core values is incompatible with your other core values and to address this incompatibility in some way, as Janine was starting to do. In this chapter, you will examine your core values and determine whether they are compatible with each other and the work–life balance outcomes you desire.

What Are Your Values?

Before you determine whether and how your values are incompatible with each other, you first need to define what your actual values are. You need to quantify your core values so you can make deliberate choices about how you want to honor these values in your daily life. If you know what is important to you, this self-knowledge will make it easier for you to make choices that create enhanced work–life balance as well as to challenge any decisions that threaten your desired work–life balance.

The text that follows includes a three-part process that will help you clarify your values. Each part of this process will contain a fieldwork exercise; as you engage in each exercise, you will gain greater clarity on your values. During this values clarification process, you will . . .

- name your values
- identify your ten most important, or core, values
- write values statements to define each of your core values.

The three fieldwork exercises for clarifying your values are somewhat involved and will probably require a good chunk of time to complete in total. Yet, I strongly encourage you not to skip any of the values exercises in this chapter because having clarity on your values—and then making choices to reflect those values—is critical to being satisfied with your choices. Of all the fieldwork I invite my clients to complete, the values-related fieldwork is the one that people report helps them make a particularly dramatic and permanent positive change in their lives.

Name Your Values: A list of possible personal values is shown in the following text. To review, a value is a belief that is extremely important to you, a quality that makes you who you are, or a principle that you uphold in how you choose to live your life. With a pen in hand, review this list and circle any values that feel meaningful and relevant to you. This list is not all-inclusive, so you will likely want to add other values that do not appear on the list that are important to you. Once you have gone through this list and circled your particular values, consider and record any values that are not on the list that are also meaningful and relevant to you. Note that you can also conduct this exercise in your *7 Keys Workbook and Journal*, or you can write down the values that are meaningful and relevant to you in your dedicated work space.

Accomplishment	Authenticity	Compassion
Accuracy	Beauty	Connectedness
Acknowledgment	Bliss	Contribution
Action	Certainty	Creativity
Advancement	Choice	Danger
Adventure	Clarity	Daring
Aesthetics	Collaboration	Design
Art	Commitment	Devotion
Attractiveness	Community	Directness

Discovery	Independence	Play
Education	Individuality	Pleasure
Elegance	Influence	Power
Empathy	Ingenuity	Prestige
Empowerment	Innovation	Productivity
Enlightenment	Integrity	Recognition
Excellence	Intimacy	Refinement
Excitement	Joy	Relationships
Exhilaration	Knowledge	Relaxation
Experience	Leadership	Religion
Experimentation	Lifelong Learning	Resilience
Expertise	Loyalty	Responsibility
Fame	Mastery	Risk Taking
Family	Meaning	Romance
Feelings	Mentoring	Self-Expression
Financial Security	Moderation	Self-Sufficiency
Flexibility	Music	Sensuality
Freedom	Nature	Serenity
Fun	Orderliness	Service
Grace	Originality	Spirituality
Harmony	Partnership	Sports
Health	Passion	Strength
Holiness	Peace	Success
Honesty	Perfection	Superiority
Honor	Performance	Systems
Humor	Persistence	Teaching
Imagination	Persuasion	Tenderness

Thrill-Seeking	Trust	Wellness
Time w/Family and Friends	Unity	Winning
Tradition	Vitality	Zest
Tranquility		

[insert your own values below, as needed]

_____   _____

_____   _____

_____   _____

_____   _____

_____   _____

_____   _____

◆   ◆   ◆

Once you have made your way through the list in the previous *Name Your Values* fieldwork exercise, you will have identified many values that are important to you—one of the important steps toward clarifying your values. If you look over this list now, how does it feel to you? If it feels reflective of you and your values, you are ready to go on to the next phase of values clarification: identifying your *core* values—the top ten most important values you hold in your life right now. If the list you created in the *Name Your Values* fieldwork exercise does not yet feel fully reflective of you, you will probably want to take some additional time to tweak it. When you are ready, you may move on to the next exercise.

Identify Your Core Values: The next step in clarifying your values is to take out your *7 Keys Workbook and Journal* or other dedicated work space and narrow your circled values from the list in the previous fieldwork (*Name Your Values*) to a "top ten" list of core values. As you engage in this narrowing process, feel free to combine two or three values together if they mean similar things to you and feel important at a core level. For example, *honesty* and *integrity* might fit on one line for you, or *knowledge* and *lifelong learning* might fit on another.

This is a tough exercise and some people feel resistant to it because it involves a forced choice in which you have to cross some important values off of your list in favor of other, more important core values. I strongly encourage you to go ahead with the exercise even if it feels difficult. Crossing a value off of your list does not mean it is no longer important to you—you are just recognizing that it is *less important* to you than other of your values at this time. This forced choice is actually an important part of the process, as you want to reflect on which of your values are the *most* significant to you. Ultimately, deciphering your core values will provide you with essential information for designing a life that is more reflective of you—and possibly of your desired work–life balance, depending on how you choose to act on the knowledge you gain regarding your values.

When you are ready, return to your circled list of values from the previous *Name Your Values* fieldwork exercise, identify the ten values (or combined values) that feel most meaningful to you and write them down in a new list.

Which values did you select? How did this process feel? Difficult? Challenging? Interesting? Enlightening? What did you learn about yourself that was new? What did you remember about yourself that perhaps you had forgotten?

If the process of selecting your ten core values flowed fairly easily for you and/or you were excited and energized by the process, you may be ready to move on to the last piece of the values clarification process—defining what each value means to you by writing what I call *personal values statements*.

If, instead, you felt resistant to the process or are still trying to get comfortable with the top ten values you selected—making sure that they are really the ones most reflective of you—consider taking a few days to try these values out in the real world. Review your ten core values as you start each day and then observe how you think, feel, and believe in relation to the unfolding events of the day to see if the core values you identified for yourself are truly reflected. If you see your values coming into play, pay attention to how you are defining a given value. If you discover that you need to make adjustments to your ten core values, go ahead and make the necessary changes to your list. Once you are ready, you can move on to the third part of the values clarification process.

 Write Your Personal Values Statements: Once you are comfortable with your top ten list of core values, you will begin defining what each value means to you by writing a personal values statement for each in your *7 Keys Workbook and Journal* or other dedicated work space. This is a very personal process, meaning that everyone defines their values differently, even when they select the same word. For example, two of my core values are passion and individuality. In all likelihood, even if you also selected passion and individuality, these values would probably mean something very different to you than they do to me.

Here are examples of how I define *passion* and *individuality* in my own personal values statements.

1. *Passion* means this to me: I feel fully and am energized by extremes. My love for my husband and son is deep and intense. My commitment to my family and friends is unbending. My work thrills me. I sob loudly, scream boldly, and laugh until I cannot catch my breath.

2. *Individuality* means this to me: I must express myself and do it freely. If I am stifled, I will not function well. I speak up, I cannot wear a uniform, I am not afraid to stand out in a crowd.

The previous two values statements represent my personal definitions of the values of passion and individuality. For someone else, passion might mean something different, for example, engaging intensely in work that the person loves. Individuality might mean having the freedom to dress in unique ways that express oneself. As you can see, people's values statements are very personal to the individual. There is no right or wrong answer when writing your personal values statements—how you craft these statements is meant to be based on whatever feels right to you.

As you engage in writing your personal values statements, I encourage you to take some time to work on your statements— several days or more. Think of your personal values statements as a work in progress that you may tweak over time. The point here is to tangibly define your values so you can then align your actions with what you have defined as being most important to you.

Once you have completed your ten personal values statements, I encourage you to put them somewhere accessible or visible to you. Post them on your refrigerator, hang them on your office wall, download them into your PDA, or carry them in your briefcase.

◆   ◆   ◆

Now that you have completed the previous three fieldwork exercises, you likely have greater awareness of your values— that is, which values are important to you, which values are your ten most significant core values, and how you define these ten core values. In other words, you have just completed some very significant work! This work can serve you now and in the future as you make choices and decisions on how to live your life in a way that reflects what is most meaningful to you.

Ultimately, knowing your values makes your priorities clearer and your decisions easier. Furthermore, when you incorporate your values into your choices and actions, the outcomes feel right. In contrast, when you disregard your values, doing so will likely feel uncomfortable and can cause anger, frustration, despair, or other negative emotions.

Thus, with awareness of your values, you will have greater understanding of some of your emotions. To see this in practice, let's return to the earlier example of working for a prestigious architectural firm that requires me to work long hours. If I feel angry every time Sunday night rolls around and the workweek is about to begin again, a look at my values might help me make sense of my anger. I might discover that I am feeling anger because a busy workweek is about to start and I know that there won't be any time for friends or recreation during the workweek—two of my core values.

Alternately, if I value prestige and passion, instead of feeling the negative emotion of anger, I might feel the positive emotion of excitement each time I walk into the lobby of my stately and highly regarded architectural firm because working at this firm supports my values.

Thus, the more clarity you have on your values, the more you are likely to understand the emotions that you experience as you put into practice (or don't put into practice!) those values in your daily life. Note that the reverse is also true. Your emotions can serve as a good barometer for whether you are enacting your values each day.

You might notice, for example, that when things feel really good—when your emotions are positive and you are operating in a state of "flow" or at optimum capacity—it is likely that you are making choices aligned with your values. When things do not feel right—when you feel disgruntled, angry, or annoyed or you do not want to be doing what you are doing—it is likely that you are not respecting your values. This means the choices you are making and the actions you are taking are not reflecting the values that are currently most meaningful and important to you.

With greater awareness of your values, you will be able to determine the compatibility of your core values with each other and with your desired work–life balance.

Identifying the Barrier: Incompatible Values

For some of you, you will find that your core values "fit" with each other and with your work–life balance preferences—that they are compatible with each other—or at least that there are no major values conflicts among them. In this case, your values do not compete with each other—they all can co-exist and be supported while you work toward your preferred work–life balance. For example, if your core values now include joy, integrity, adventure, health, romance, accomplishment, and knowledge and you currently have work and a personal life that honors all of these values, your core values are currently compatible with each other. As you review what these actually mean to you in your personal values statements, you do not notice any mismatches between these values and your work–life desires. That is, your vision of ideal work–life balance involves occasional vacations in the outdoors (adventure), finding time to date (romance), and being in a career that makes you feel happy every day (joy). Therefore, the *incompatible-values* barrier is likely not getting in the way of your work–life balance satisfaction.

In contrast, if you discover that one or more of your core values are being honored right now at the expense of another of your core value or values, this means that your values are currently incompatible with each other and that you face the incompatible-values barrier. That is, you are not able to support and honor all of these values at the same time—or, at least, your current work–life situation makes it difficult for you to do so.

For example, let's imagine that your core values include passion, devotion, community, fame, leadership, independence, perfection, and health. Upon closer reflection of what these values mean to you and how they are expressed in your actions, you see that your focus on fame, passion, and leadership are driving current career choices more than your desire for a different work–life balance situation. If this is the case, incompatible values is one of the barriers you face on your journey to work–life balance.

To be clear, the incompatible-values barrier can take shape in three different forms.

- An incompatibility exists between one or more of my core values and my current work-life situation (e.g., I have a core value of orderliness, but I work so many hours that I am unable to keep my house tidy or organized).

- An incompatibility exists between one or more of my core values and my preferred work–life balance (e.g., I have a core value of entrepreneurship so I spend most of my time on my current business and thinking of new business ideas, not letting myself train for a marathon, which is a big part of my preferred work–life balance).

- An incompatibility exists between the values themselves (I want two different things, e.g., I value achievement *and* romance, but my current job, which fulfills my desire for achievement, keeps me so busy that I do not have time to date).

Whichever form the incompatibility takes, once this barrier of incompatible values is acknowledged, you then have choices on how to proceed. Later in the text, those choices will be defined. First, let's take some time to reflect on your core values and whether they work against your desired work–life balance.

Common Pitfalls That Lead to Incompatible Values

As you prepare to delve deeper into possible values incompatibilities, consider these common pitfalls (these are just some—you may discover your own, too) and try to observe which ones, if any, sound familiar. Note that each situation involves values that are incompatible with a person's desired work–life balance and that these incompatible values drive the person to make decisions or stay in situations that keep him or her feeling unbalanced and dissatisfied.

Golden handcuffs. You would like more balance in your life, but you feel you are wearing "golden handcuffs," meaning that you feel as if you are a prisoner to your job and its salary. You believe you cannot leave your current position because you are compensated very well and you will lose significant benefits and investments if you make any changes that will jeopardize your current position. Furthermore, you believe you cannot even consider looking for other employment as no other company could afford you at the current salary you are making. The stronger values in this situation may include financial security, prestige, or advancement.

Adrenaline junkie. You thrive on adrenaline, urgency, and always doing. You like the intensity of your work even though you are aware of the adverse repercussions in terms of your desired work–life balance. Here, values of adventure, exhilaration, excitement, or thrill-seeking may take precedence over your desired work–life balance.

Success equals feeling overwhelmed. You equate feeling overwhelmed with accomplishment and success. You assume that all successful people are just really busy and that the feeling of being overwhelmed is a problem that can be tackled by working even more and harder. Your values of persistence, devotion, loyalty, or productivity may override your desired work–life balance state.

Means to an end. You accept lack of balance as a means to an end, although there is no end in sight. This shows up by you often thinking to yourself, "it will only be this way for another month, three months, six months." But, over time, the pace never slows down and the situation never changes on its own, as something else always arises to keep you at your current level of busy-ness and commitment, thus preventing meaningful change. Other stronger values are enabling you to push off work–life balance as something to address in the future.

These are just a few examples of the pitfalls that make it easy to maintain values that are incompatible with your preferred work–life balance. Did you find yourself having any "aha!" moments as you read through the examples? Or perhaps you realized that some other way of thinking or operating has kept you in a situation where the values you are living are incompatible with the direction in which you would like to take your life for enhanced work–life balance.

Once you are aware of which of your values are driving your current behavior, you can make different choices or you can more readily accept your current state.

 Discover Your Incompatible Values: Let's take some time now to review the personal values statements you wrote earlier in the chapter (see the *Write Your Personal Values Statements* fieldwork), with an eye to identifying any incompatible values. With your personal values statements in mind, think about your current and desired work–life balance. This would be a good time to take out the three-word descriptor you created for yourself in the first chapter of the book (*A Road Map for the Journey: How Satisfied Are You?;* see the *Describe Your Preferred Work–Life Balance Situation* fieldwork).

The goal here is to think about the values you are living right now versus the values inherent in your desired work–life balance. After you have spent some time reflecting on the compatibility or incompatibility of your values with your desired work–life situation, write down all of the incompatibilities you have discovered. In particular, you will want to …

- write down the dominating value(s) that currently serve(s) as a barrier to your desired–work life balance

- identify the decisions you make and the actions you take (or do not take) to support this value

- write down the name of the value(s) you are sacrificing in order to support the dominant value and describe how your desired work–life balance could be supported by changing your behavior to honor the "sacrificed" value.

For example, you might write the following statements as you identify your values incompatibilities.

- *My value of financial security stops me from pursuing a degree in teaching because I fear I won't make enough money. But teaching would support my values of leadership and helping others, as well as provide more work–life balance because I'd have summers off (which would support my value of family time).*

- *My value of family time is conflicting with my value of leadership in my profession. Because I value family time, I turn down opportunities to attend professional conferences and networking events. Yet, if I attended more of these events, my desired work–life state of being more engaged at work would be more fulfilled as I would be developing myself professionally and preparing for future leadership roles.*

- *My values of perfection and achievement at work are steering my time and energy away from my nonprofessional values of music and relationships because I'm too busy with work to find time to play music or to see friends. My preferred state of work–life balance involves me finding a group of musicians with whom to do regular jam sessions and going out with friends at least one night a week, which would help me support my values of music and relationships.*

As you can see from the previous examples, as your values are more clearly defined, you can identify where values incompatibilities exist—whether between two of your core values themselves or between one of your core values and your desired work–life balance. You can also begin to identify values changes and behavioral changes that might support your desired work–life balance (more on that later in the chapter).

If you feel comfortable sharing this information with someone else, you may want to work with that person as a partner on this exercise. Ask a significant other, friend, or trusted colleague who knows you well to talk through this exercise with you. Share your personal values statements as well as your desired work–life balance state. Ask the person if he or she sees any incompatibilities between your values, actions, and work–life balance preferences. Having external perspective on this very personal situation may assist you in seeing values incompatibilities that you might otherwise miss.

◆   ◆   ◆

Armed with your new awareness of your values incompatibilities, you can now choose the best path to move forward and the changes you are willing to make, if any.

Putting the Key Into Practice

If you would like to overcome the barrier of incompatible values, you will need to either

- accept the values incompatibility or
- reprioritize your values preferences.

In the first case, you acknowledge the values incompatibility, accept it, and choose to continue living with it (for now, anyway). For example, if the values of peace and calm are very important to you, but you work at a job that keeps you so busy and stressed that you never feel peace and calm, you might choose to accept this stress and lack of peace and calm if you realize this sacrifice is worth it to you right now for the trade–off it offers you in terms of having a job that fulfills your value of contribution. This option equates to accepting the status quo.

When you reprioritize your values preferences, you shift your emphasis from one core value onto another. In particular, you place greater emphasis on a core value that was previously less supported by you and, at the same time, place lesser emphasis on a currently dominant core value. For example, you might decide that peace and calm are more important to you right now than your value of contribution. Once you make this mental shift to reprioritize your values, you will be able to make different choices about what kind of work you do. As a result, you might start looking for a new job or you might try to negotiate a different schedule or workload with your boss. When you reprioritize your values, your behavior changes as a result.

Being aware of your values incompatibilities will allow you to either accept what is or make a change.

Choosing the Status Quo

In reviewing your values incompatibilities, you may discover that your desired work–life balance may not be attainable with your current core values. If you choose to accept this situation, you are choosing the status quo and the lifestyle and repercussions that go with it. Let's return to the earlier example of incompatible values in which you discovered that your value of family time is making it difficult for you to support your value of leadership at work (see the *Discover Your Incompatible Values* fieldwork). After recognizing this incompatibility, you might still choose to remain with the status quo—turning down professional development and networking opportunities in favor of having more time with your spouse and kids.

In cases in which you choose the status quo, you are either unwilling or unable to make behavior changes due to your strong values. As a result, you choose to retain your current, more unbalanced way of operating. This is a completely acceptable response, as long as you are making this choice deliberately and are comfortable with the potential consequences.

An important thing to remember if you do choose to continue with a situation of incompatible values is to commit to a finite time frame in this state. Then, schedule a time on your calendar for another review and evaluation in the future. For example, in the case of family time eclipsing leadership, you might re-evaluate the situation once your children have moved on to the next phase of development (e.g., reached school age, started high school, or gone off to college—depending on their age). You might also choose a six- or twelve-month time frame to evaluate whether the status quo is no longer working, even before a phase of your life has ended. Your comfort or discomfort with the situation can change anytime, so allow yourself to evaluate the current situation based on your comfort level, too.

Here is another example of how someone might choose the status quo when faced with incompatible values.

Nancy, an attorney, has been working on a lucrative, highly visible case for her Firm. Over the next six months, she will lead a team to take this case to trial. If she and the team are successful, the financial rewards for the client, and therefore for her Firm, are significant, setting her up for certain promotion to Partner. This promotion has been a professional goal of Nancy's for the past eight years and she believes it will acknowledge her talents and give her the job security and financial rewards she desires. Nancy is choosing to work very long hours and have extensive time away from her family, friends, and normal routine in order to achieve success with this case and also with her desired professional path (in order to support her values of achievement and advancement).

Nancy knows that her next six months will be nowhere near supportive of her preferred way of living and working and that she is choosing to honor a set of values that are incompatible with her desire for more time with friends and family (her work–life balance preferences). Nancy's unbalanced state and incompatible values feel acceptable to her, though, because she is aware of her incompatible values and is making a deliberate choice around her values and actions and because she feels that the sacrifice is worth the reward. Once this case is over, Nancy can take some time to re-evaluate whether she would like to make changes in her life to align her current work–life situation with a different core value (or values).

Reprioritizing Your Values

Another approach when you discover incompatible values is to look at the two values that are competing with each other—that are incompatible—and choose to put greater emphasis on the one you have not been supporting and to put less emphasis on the one that has been taking precedence. In essence, you can reprioritize your core values, giving a higher priority to one and a lesser priority to another. (This process can also occur with more than two values, but I have used the example of two for the sake of simplicity and clarity.) Once you make this mental reprioritization of your values, your behavior may then change as a result of this mental shift. This values reprioritization— followed by a behavior change supportive of that values reprioritization—will help move you forward on your path toward your preferred work–life balance.

For example, Max, a chef at a four-star restaurant, might decide that community involvement has become more important to him than the prestige he garners in his career as a top city chef. As a result, he might start looking for a position at a restaurant that serves only breakfast and lunch so he has his evenings free for getting more involved in neighborhood and city activities. If this occurs, Max will have *reprioritized his values*, de-emphasizing his value of prestige in favor of supporting his value of community involvement.

In sum, when you reprioritize your values, you allow a new value (that more directly supports your desired work–life balance) to take prominence over another value that has until now been driving your choices and behavior in your current situation. Perhaps the de-emphasized value still gets supported but to a lesser degree; or perhaps you decide to stop supporting it altogether.

Reprioritizing one's values is likely to lead to significant changes that impact both work and life. For Max, reprioritizing his values meant that he might no longer receive coveted write-ups in the city newspaper since he would be moving to a less prestigious food establishment. Yet, it also meant that he would have the time he desires to focus on greater involvement in his community. Max gives up something, but he gains something in return and moves closer to his desired work–life balance in the process.

External Factors That Can Spur a Values Reprioritization

Unfortunately, many of us often wait to deal with incompatible values until we are forced to do so—through external challenges or major life crises. This was the case in the earlier example of Janine, in which a health problem caused her to make some changes in her life. There are a variety of other external factors that might require someone to deal with incompatible values. They include the following.

Pain, either physical or emotional. You hurt your back, leading to constant physical discomfort. Your core value of accomplishment now takes a back seat to your need to care for yourself. You are no longer as focused on needing to be the top sales executive in your company. You make health, healing, and physical fitness core values as you overcome this challenge.

Change of life status. Marriage, divorce, the birth of a new child, or the death of a loved one often causes a re-evaluation of what is important in life and therefore in work. If you are a parent with a new child, you may no longer be willing to work 70-hour workweeks. Previous to the child, your core values may have included professional recognition and adventure. Your new family status altered your core values to include family, stability, and relationships. A divorce might cause reflection and awareness that the values of success, superiority, and adventure were not congruent with maintaining your marriage. As you commit to a new relationship, you work toward integrating your values of responsibility, commitment, and family.

Unexpected events. These events, including accidents, tragedies, getting fired, or winning the lottery, can immediately change your core values. Losing a job unexpectedly might cause someone to embrace the values of creativity and experimentation. Because the "golden handcuffs" of a job have been removed, the person might decide to "go for it" and try a new profession, trading financial security for creative fulfillment. Someone who has lost her home to a natural disaster might be catalyzed to de-emphasize her value of material wealth and place a greater emphasis, instead, on spirituality. As a result, she may start spending more time at her place of worship, which might move her closer to her desired work–life balance, in which she dedicates more time to her spiritual life and her community.

In each of these situations, individuals have reprioritized their values as a reaction to external factors or outside events. While this reaction of making changes in the face of uncomfortable externalities is an effective coping mechanism and I applaud my clients who are able to make such changes, I still encourage those with less dramatic circumstances to consider making the changes necessary to deal with incompatible values before an external factor forces the issue. Why wait to be sick before pursuing more balance? Why wait until tragedy strikes to be motivated to change?

Instead of allowing life circumstances to steer your values, you can take a thoughtful, planned approach to reprioritizing your core values.

Although choosing the status quo is always an option for handling incompatible values, the discovery of incompatible values also provides you with a valuable opportunity to move closer to your desired work–life balance. Since you likely picked up this book because of some dissatisfaction you were feeling in regard to your current work–life balance, I encourage you to spend some time exploring ways that you might be able to make adjustments to your values or behaviors rather than simply accepting the status quo. Now may or may not be the right time to reprioritize your values, but give yourself a chance to truly explore rather than automatically sticking with what is familiar.

 To Reprioritize or to Accept? You have defined your values and identified your incompatibilities. Now it is time to decide what to do about what you have discovered. Let's start with what you choose to change. In your *7 Keys Workbook and Journal* or other dedicated work space, describe each values reprioritization that you want to make and the resulting behavior change that will go with it. The following represent examples of what you might write down.

> *Value Reprioritization*: from perfection → to competence
> *Behavior Change*: from staying up until 3 a.m. "wordsmithing" a report → to deciding it is good enough. I will tell myself, "I am a good writer and my boss will be satisfied with my work, or she will give me feedback to improve it."

> *Value Reprioritization*: from loyalty → to self-sufficiency
> *Behavior Change*: from continuing to work with a longtime boss who has unreasonable expectations on my working hours and who allows for no flexibility → to communicating directly to my boss about my professional and personal needs and considering an external job search, if necessary.

Once you have quantified your values reprioritization and have defined specific behaviors you plan to change, I encourage you to decide when you will commit to this new action (ideally, in the next week or so in order to keep your momentum going) by writing down the date or adding it to your schedule or calendar. When that date approaches, go ahead and integrate one behavior change and notice the results and how you feel. Continue with this process as your actions become compatible with your values.

Finally, be aware that making any change can take time. You may need time to get comfortable with the actual behavior change and time to notice and enjoy the resulting benefits. You are likely shifting a value and a behavior that you have held for a long time and that may have been useful to you up to this point. So, be aware that this process does not happen overnight and it does not always feel easy at first. This process takes commitment, practice, diligence, and regular re-evaluation. As you begin to reprioritize your values so they are more compatible with your desired work–life balance—and make related behavioral changes—you are likely to find yourself moving toward your desired work–life balance.

- A value is a belief that is extremely important to you, a quality that makes you who you are, or a principle that you uphold on how you choose to live your life.
- Defining your core values provides you with valuable information for designing a life that is more reflective of who you are—and possibly of your desired work–life balance, depending on how you choose to act on that knowledge (accepting the status quo vs. reprioritizing your values).
- When there is incompatibility between your values and your actions, you may feel anger, frustration, despair, or other negative emotions.
- When your values and the actions you take are compatible or complementary, you feel positive, energized, excited, or in flow.
- Create a regular interval of time to review your ten personal values statements (for example, every three to six months). At these intervals, ask yourself if you are respecting your values and making choices that are compatible with your values.
- Your values preferences may change over time or due to life events. Allow for appropriate changes in your choices and actions to reflect these factors.

- Pain, change of life status (marriage, divorce, births, deaths), and unexpected events can often lead to a quick values reprioritization.
- Values incompatibilities will happen. Pause. Reflect. And make choices that lead to a greater expression of your values. This is how you will find greater satisfaction in work and in life.
- At times, you may choose to live with a values incompatibility. If you make this choice, be aware of the consequences and select a length of time until you will re-evaluate your choices and values.
- You can reprioritize your values preference to more accurately reflect what matters to you; then you can adjust your behavior to match your values. Depending on your circumstances, a values reprioritization—followed by a behavior change—can move you toward your desired work–life balance.

KEY 6

Navigate an Unbalanced Organizational Culture

So far in the book, the focus has largely been on you—your priorities; your boundaries; your time, energy, and attention; your expectations; and your values. In the process, you have acknowledged and considered your interactions with other people—because none of us lives in a vacuum—but in large part, the book so far has had you looking inward and then making appropriate choices for you and taking action. This approach in the book has been purposeful because for most people who struggle with work–life balance, their tendency is to focus too much on *everyone else's* needs, requests, or demands—whether at work, in the community, or at home—rather than on themselves and their own priorities.

Thus, as has become more clear chapter by chapter, to pursue your ideal work–life balance, you need to start placing more focus on you and your preferences. That being said, I also realize that you live in the real world. No matter how clear you are on your priorities, your boundaries, your expectations, and your values, you will be spending a lot of your time moderating these things within the context of the organizations and communities in which you work, interact, volunteer, operate, and live.

The truth is that the environment in which you dwell at any given time has a big impact on your ability to foster work–life balance. Some environments are favorable to work–life balance, while others tend to inhibit your ability to move toward work–life balance.

This chapter will provide you with an opportunity to look outward and assess the nature of the organizations and communities in which you operate. You will be asking, are the cultural norms of these organizations and communities conducive to your desired work–life balance? In other words, do they support balance? Or do they make it difficult for you to put into action your plans for things like maintaining priorities, creating boundaries, and setting reasonable expectations? In other words, are they unsupportive of balance?

In sum, this chapter will help you assess whether the organizations and communities in which you participate are supportive or unsupportive of balance, contemplate what kinds of changes you may want to make to address environments that are unsupportive of balance, and then implement a plan to make adjustments to bring more balance into your life, whether by changing the organizational culture or choosing to disengage from that culture and find a new one more supportive to you.

Developing Awareness of the Key

A Closer Look at the Concept

An *unbalanced organizational culture* means that the structures, policies, expectations, and/or history of the organization do not support creating an environment in which work–life balance is a concern, a priority, or even a possibility. There are a lot of terms in that definition, so I will define those, too:

- **organization** – a group of which you are a part and where you spend some of your time
- **culture** – written or unwritten operating rules to which most members of the organization subscribe.

In light of these two definitions, let's go over the definition of unbalanced organizational culture again: When the group to which you belong has written or unwritten operating rules that do not support the creation of an environment in which work–life balance is considered, valued, or implemented, you are faced with an unbalanced organizational culture. Note that although the book thus far has used the term *balance* in a subjective sense that is meant to be defined by each individual, in the case of organizations, there are some objective criteria that can be observed to point to whether the culture is supportive or unsupportive of balance.

Some examples of an unbalanced organizational culture include the following:

- The organization's leadership does not value balance for their employees by not having any policies or procedures in place for creating flexibility or choices for how employees work.
- "Face time" is expected of employees, meaning you need to be seen in your office even when you are not providing value or you could be working productively elsewhere.
- Leaders of the organization possess a mentality of "needing to pay your dues," meaning that this is the way others before you have done it, so you have to do it this way, too.

- The organization operates with an "in loco parentis" perspective, in which the organization or your supervisor takes on a parental role, wanting to know where you are at all times, what you are doing, and why you are doing it and wants to give input into all of your choices. Therefore, you have no flexibility or autonomy with designing your own schedule or way of working/operating.

An unbalanced organizational culture can manifest itself in a variety of ways. The previous descriptions represent some of the common forms in which an unbalanced organizational culture often becomes evident.

Now let's look at an example of someone who faced an unbalanced organizational culture to gain more insight into what an unbalanced culture might look like.

Frank worked for a large management consulting firm in which he was very successful. He was promoted to a Partner, enjoyed his work, and managed his very hectic schedule of 80% travel and 100% availability to his clients. After his son was born, though, Frank began to feel unhappy with being away from home so much and was losing his energy and excitement for his work. After about a year, Frank decided that he did not want to continue at the level of traveling that kept him away from his son so often. After lots of reflection, he approached various leaders in the Firm as well as Human Resources to determine how to lessen his travel. He was even willing to work a reduced 60% time schedule and take the matching salary cut. The Firm was not willing to reduce his time or travel as Frank was working on large and financially lucrative clients who wanted him on location. With this response, and more personal reflection and discussions, Frank decided to resign from his position, as the Firm was not supportive of finding a way in which to address Frank's new needs as a father.

In this case, the Firm's unwillingness to reduce Frank's work or travel time—or to brainstorm on other solutions—was a sign that the organizational culture was unbalanced. In other words, the Firm's culture was not conducive to allowing Frank to bring more balance into his own life. It did not allow the creation of an environment in which work–life balance was considered, valued, or implemented.

I want to be careful to acknowledge here that readers may have differing opinions on whether the Firm's response was fair, reasonable, or appropriate. Some might argue that this was a very reasonable response given the nature of the Firm's business; others might argue that the Firm's approach was inflexible or outmoded. My goal in this chapter when referring to organizational cultures as unbalanced is not to place any value judgments on organizations but instead to exemplify the criteria used to make up the definition of unbalanced organizational culture presented earlier in the chapter. Ultimately, I will be encouraging you to assess on an individual basis whether your organization's culture is unbalanced given your own picture of ideal work–life balance and then to decide when and if and how you would like to make changes to address this lack of balance.

Up to this point in the chapter, when speaking of organizations, I have meant employers. Yet, your family is also an organization that may not always (or at all) support your work–life balance needs. Other organizations to consider when you read this chapter include organizations in which you volunteer time, such as religious institutions, professional associations, volunteer organizations, and community associations.

Identifying the Barrier: Unbalanced Organizational Culture

When you belong to an organization with an unbalanced culture, your life can be affected in a number of ways. For example, you may find it difficult to carve out quality time to spend with your family, you may encounter difficulty developing a healthy exercise routine, or you might find it challenging to participate in community activities. These are just some of the negative consequences that can result from your belonging to an organization with an unbalanced culture. Whatever your picture of ideal work–life balance, an *unbalanced organizational culture* can serve as a barrier to your moving closer to that ideal.

Now let's look at some specific examples of how the culture of organizations can impact a person's work–life balance. As you read through these descriptions, pay attention to whether any of the situations sound familiar to your own life and the organizations, institutions, and communities in which you operate.

Tenure or Bust

The first example involves Colleen, a university professor.

> Colleen is hoping to achieve tenure over the next few years. Her university's expectations for professors to achieve tenure include that they meet significant publishing requirements, chair various committees, supervise graduate and undergraduate student research projects, hold office hours, be very responsive to student needs, and continue to excel at their teaching responsibilities. In addition, the more senior tenured faculty members in Colleen's department continue to pass on additional work to her as she is the most junior person in the department. As such, Colleen finds

that her work is all-encompassing. Not surprisingly, she sees her other tenure-focused colleagues experiencing the same high work-load. As she starts to reflect on the organizational culture, she real-izes that there is no concern or empathy for this heavy workload, nor is there any opportunity to change the "system." Instead, she simply hears from others, "grin and bare it ... this is the hell of tenure. You'll get to watch others go through it after you're done."

In the case of Colleen, she is faced with an organizational culture that possesses a "pay your dues" mentality. This leaves her to struggle with whether the joy she finds in teaching is strong enough to support her through the grueling process of tenure that she is unable to change.

Never Leave Before the Boss

Now let's examine the case of David.

David is a recent college graduate who started working in an investment-banking firm in New York City. David, who prides himself on efficiency and working hard, is aware that he will have very long hours and that at times he will "pull all-nighters" when important deadlines are approaching. He is comfortable with the intense nature of the business. He has noticed a strange pattern, though. It seems that every evening, regardless of the workload, no one on his team leaves the office before their managing director. Even when people have finished their work for the evening, they keep themselves busy until the director says goodbye, and then the entire floor empties. David has found himself doing busywork for one to two hours some nights, when he could be at home sleeping or out with friends.

In this case, David is dealing with the consequences of the organizational cultural norm of "face time." This leaves him feeling very frustrated as he regularly completes his responsibilities and would prefer to pursue other activities in his evenings but is concerned about what may happen or how he may be perceived by others if he steps outside of this norm.

Two Full-Time Jobs

Lisa represents someone else who is faced with an unbalanced organizational culture.

> Lisa owns and operates a very successful executive recruiting firm. This keeps her very busy meeting with clients, interviewing candidates, attending professional meetings, and more. She is also a mother of three, who is active in her children's school and extracurricular events; she is typically able to schedule her "mom time" around her professional commitments. Her husband is a busy executive who travels frequently, leaving him gone during most weeks and exhausted during the weekends. With her busy schedule at work and with her kids, and her husband too tired to help on weekends, Lisa rarely has "downtime." Instead, in her spare time, she is occupied planning meals for the week, grocery shopping, cooking, running all sorts of errands, and meeting the needs of her kids and husband. On the rare occasion when she gets sick, she feels like a house of cards has fallen, leaving her with a huge mess to clean up once she is able, and then it takes at least a few weeks to get back to where things are running again. She is constantly concerned that something will go wrong and she might not be able to keep things afloat either professionally or personally.

In this case, Lisa has the equivalent of two full-time jobs— one as an executive recruiter, the other as a mom who does it all. The "organizational culture" of her family is not structured to provide Lisa with anything that even approaches her desired work–life balance. Her family life has always operated this way, but Lisa no longer feels able to manage the resultant stress, worry, and sleepless nights.

Professional Association Overload

Lastly, let's look at the case of Graham.

> Graham is a marketing manager for a bicycle manufacturer. He loves his work as he is able to combine his professional skills and interests with his passion for cycling. He even gets time off to train for long-distance bike races. This year he decided to take on the role of president of the regional marketing professional association, a personal commitment outside of his work role that nonetheless can enhance the respect he receives from others in his professional field. Although Graham thought this responsibility would entail about five hours per month of administrative work and meetings, a few months into the position, he is discovering that many more hours are required. In addition, a few of the board members of his association are not upholding their commitments, leaving Graham to pick up the slack. He feels strongly as president that if the organization does not look good, he will not be seen as the leader in his field that he prides himself to be. Yet, Graham is feeling completely overwhelmed with his association responsibilities, when added to his current work responsibilities, and he is no longer able to spend time on his bike. He is not sure if he can continue working in this unbalanced organizational culture as it is throwing off his desired work–life balance.

In this case, the unbalanced organizational culture that Graham is facing is within a professional association in which he chose to volunteer his time. He is struggling with this commitment he made as it is having unintended consequences on his nonwork activities that are very important to him.

Do any of the previous stories sound familiar to you? The following fieldwork exercise will provide you with an opportunity to assess whether any of the organizations in which you operate have an unbalanced culture.

Evaluate Your Organizations: Now that you have an understanding of the meaning of unbalanced organizational culture and you have seen some of the ways that this barrier can impact work–life balance, take some time to reflect on the balanced or unbalanced nature of the organizations to which you belong. Over the next week, pay attention to how the organizations in which you are involved operate in terms of their ability to foster or inhibit work–life balance. In particular, observe organizational policies and procedures, expectations, and unwritten rules and think about how they promote or impede your desired work–life balance. Notice, too, how the choices of other members of the organization impact your work–life balance. As you engage in this exercise, consider each of the organizations to which you belong—for example, the company where you work, organizations where you volunteer, professional associations, and your family.

At the end of the week, pull out your *7 Keys Workbook and Journal* or other dedicated work space and answer the following questions for each organization in which you are involved.

- How does my organization sabotage my work–life balance preferences or not support them?
- What is the impact of this situation on me?

For example, David's response to these questions might be ...

This past week at work, on three different nights I stayed one to two hours after I completed my project work for the day. My workday should have ended then. But I stayed and caught up with my email and actually spent time on my Facebook account just because no one had left the office yet. As the newest and most junior person on staff, I felt uncomfortable leaving. Besides, no one else was leaving. I pride myself on productivity, but other people must be dealing with this, too. It's impacting me as I'm not only frustrated by staying late for what feels like no reason, but I'm missing time when I could be at the gym, hanging out with my friends, or just relaxing.

In this case, David notes that the organizational culture of staying late even when he is done with his work is eating into what could be his free time outside of work. He then goes on to note the resultant impact that this unbalanced organizational culture is having on his life: it is causing him to miss exercise time, social time, and time for relaxation.

Take some time now to reflect on the organizations to which you belong. Identify which ones are sabotaging your work–life balance preferences, and what impact each situation of unbalanced organizational culture is having on you.

Now that you have identified the organizations with unbalanced culture to which you belong and the work–life balance challenges you face as a result, we will look at ways to address these challenges.

Putting the Key Into Practice

Organizational cultures and norms develop over a long period of time, and organizational change is often slow and met with significant resistance. With that said, if you want to improve your work–life balance and have identified that one or more of your organizations are making this difficult, you need to take action in some capacity.

The action you ultimately engage in to navigate organizational challenges to work–life balance can take a variety of forms. For example, you might decide to speak up within your organization and ask management to adjust organizational policies to promote more work–life balance. You might engage in a personal experiment and simply make changes on your own and see if the organization is accepting of these changes. You might even realize that you want to exit the organization and look for a different one that is better suited to your work–life preferences. Or, you might take only a minor action—by deliberately choosing to accept the situation for a while because you feel that the trade–off you are making in terms of your desired work–life balance is worth it for the gains you receive by staying in the organization. This is the technique of choosing the status quo, which was discussed in depth in the previous chapter and is also discussed later in the current chapter.

Answering the following questions will aid you in the process of deciding in which actions you will engage to navigate the barrier of unbalanced organizational culture. You will need to answer the following questions regarding each of the organizations of which you are a part and that you have identified as negatively impacting your work–life balance.

Is the Challenge Temporary or Permanent?

First, is the situation temporary or permanent? Organizations go through cycles and events that can impact what the organization needs and expects from its employees. For example, a tax accountant expects that her work–life balance will not be optimal in the weeks leading up to April 15 (in the U.S., this is the annual tax-filing deadline.) Being aware of cyclical patterns or busy periods enables you to prepare for the repercussions of an overwhelming, but temporary, workload. If the challenge is temporary, you may decide you are willing to accept a defined period of compromised work–life balance because you have adequate work–life balance the rest of the year. In contrast, if the challenge appears to be permanent, you may choose to address the challenge with a specific action plan.

Is the Challenge Situational?

Second, do you experience challenges only in some situations and not in others? For example, a project manager at the same level as you has been unfairly allocating project responsibilities that require you to work excessively on nights and weekends, while other peers are still leaving the office by 6 p.m. Determining that the challenge is situational will help you home in on where you might want to focus your efforts to resolve the challenge—for example, at the level of your boss rather than with HR. Before asking this question, you might have the feeling that your organization is not the right fit for your work–life balance. After answering this question, though, you may realize that some tweaks to your immediate situation could go a long way to improve your desired work–life balance.

To Speak up or Not to Speak up?

Finally, can you raise your voice at your organization? Are individual concerns valued or discouraged within the organization? Is someone who raises a concern seen as a contributor and problem solver, or a whiner and complainer? Before you raise a concern at your organization, you must consider how you may be perceived and whether you might experience any professional repercussions against you as a result of your candor. Depending on the patterns you have seen, you may choose to address the challenge within the organization, you may decide to say nothing and deal with the work–life imbalance for a period of time to meet some of your goals, or you may decide to leave the organization altogether.

If you determine that the organizational challenge is not (a) temporary or (b) situational and that (c) it is okay to speak up within your organization, you can then choose to address your concern. If you do want to attempt to improve the unbalanced organizational culture, I suggest you bring up your concerns to the appropriate person/people in a solution-oriented manner. By solution-oriented, I mean giving possible resolutions to your concern, not just complaining or highlighting your discomfort. This allows you to be seen as a collaborative and creative problem solver, rather than as a defensive, dissatisfied, or disillusioned employee. Ideally, you do not want to burn bridges while addressing your challenges as the organization may not be able to adequately address your concern and you may still want to be part of that organization.

In the process of creating a solution-oriented plan, consider how the changes you are suggesting will add value to the organization, and plan to highlight these as you ask for change. For example, some possibilities include ...

- quantify how telecommuting two days a week will impact your productivity at work
- show how investing in technology can not only lessen your travel requirements but lessen expenses

- engage your partner and other family members in taking on more responsibilities that will allow for more fun together on weekends
- address with the leadership of your volunteer organization how creating manageable volunteer commitments for everyone will increase the number of volunteers for the entire organization.

By highlighting the value that your requested changes are likely to bring to the organization, you will have a useful technique for getting other members of the organization invested in supporting your requested change.

The next step in navigating an unbalanced organizational culture—whether at work, at home, or elsewhere—is to quantify how much time you are willing to give to each of the organizations in your life. How you choose to allocate your time with each of your organizations will enable you to gain greater control over the impact the organization has on your work–life satisfaction. By defining in advance how much time you can give to each of your organizations and in what capacity you plan to use this time, it will make it easier to set boundaries around and create a more optimal "relationship" with your organizations.

Know Your Time Limits: To create time limits based on the number of hours you are willing to commit to your organizations, consider maximum work hours per day or per week, how much work you will do at home, amount of work and personal travel per week or month (visits to friends and family add up!), what volunteer commitments fit with your other responsibilities, and, for parents, how much carpooling is humanly possible. These are just a few areas to consider; define whatever time limits are relevant to your situation. You can then write down your desired time limits in your *7 Keys Workbook and Journal* or other dedicated work space. For example, you might write the following.

> ***My work time limits:*** *I will spend no more than a half hour per evening on work-related activities after I leave the office, Monday through Thursday.*

> ***My home/family time limits:*** *I will do three hours of house errands on the weekend and ask other members of my family to do additional needed tasks.*

> ***My other organizational time limits:*** *I will contribute five hours per month as secretary of the board of my local professional association.*

You can use the time limits you set as a benchmark to facilitate action. When you are clear on your time limits and you notice them consistently being surpassed, you can then choose to act.

You are now ready to begin creatively thinking about reframing and/or redesigning your relationship with your organization(s). You are aware of the work–life challenges that result from the unbalanced culture of the organizations to which you belong as well as the impact that these challenges have on you and your work–life balance. In addition, you have just defined more optimal time limits. Next, how might you propose new ways of operation with your organization(s)? Before engaging in a fieldwork exercise to do so, let's revisit the examples from earlier in the chapter to see various ways to address the challenging situations.

Leave the Organization and Find a New One

One way to handle an unbalanced organizational culture is to leave that culture. Colleen, the professor, ultimately decided to handle the unbalanced organizational culture of her university in just that way.

> Challenged with the culture of tenure, Colleen decided her current workload was not sustainable for her desired work–life balance over the next two to three years when she would be evaluated for tenure. She approached her department chair to discuss other options besides continuing at her current level of intensity. Where she was hoping to creatively brainstorm other possibilities, she was met with no flexibility. This left Colleen with a difficult decision—to sacrifice the next two to three years of her desired work–life balance to win possible tenure or to look elsewhere. Ultimately, Colleen decided that at this point in her life, work–life balance was more important than tenure. Since her greatest love was teaching undergraduate students rather than fulfilling the other tenure requirements at her current university, such as publishing, she began a job search focusing on smaller, teaching-focused colleges.

Although Colleen first attempted to navigate the university's unbalanced organizational culture by staying within it and requesting some changes, she was met with resistance and ultimately decided the best way for her to handle the situation was to leave the organization. If you find the expectations and operating norms of your current organizational situation too dissatisfying, frustrating, painful, and/or overwhelming, you may similarly choose to look elsewhere.

A Last Attempt: "Firing" Your Boss

If you do decide that you are willing to leave the organization, you may want to consider making one last attempt to bring about changes to the organizational culture, while working under the premise that you plan to "fire" your boss if he or she is unwilling to make any changes. You do this figuratively, not literally, by taking the mental leap that you have nothing to lose and can therefore ask for whatever you want regardless of the consequences. This last ditch effort will allow you to address your concerns without worrying about the results of your actions, and may surprisingly have a significant impact. For example...

> After trying numerous ways to navigate the twenty-four-hour on-call mentality at the hospital where he worked, senior administrator Lawrence decided he would resign. His boss was unwilling to make adjustments to the culture and even gave Lawrence negative feedback for making some adjustments on his own to improve his work–life balance. Nonetheless, before Lawrence submitted his letter of resignation, he decided to have one final conversation with his boss. Since he was content with his decision to resign, he went assertively into his boss's office and told him that he was planning to give notice in the next week unless significant changes could be made in the ways in which he was expected to complete his responsibilities. His boss was shocked to hear this as Lawrence was a very valued employee and he asked Lawrence what was required to keep Lawrence on staff. Although a little frustrated that his boss did not respond to previous concerns, Lawrence produced a document with three changes he needed to see in order to remain. The boss agreed to two of the three items and said he would look at making the third happen over the next three months. This was enough to change Lawrence's mind to stay at the hospital for at least the short-term.

Of course, Lawrence's boss could have also easily accepted Lawrence's resignation and had him pack his desk and leave the office by the end of the day. He might have questioned Lawrence's commitment to the hospital and to the field of health care. That is why the "firing" your boss method is only best used when you are truly and sincerely ready to leave the organization. When using this technique, you need to be prepared for whatever may happen.

Conduct an Experiment to Change the Organizational Culture

Sometimes, it is not necessary to leave the organization in order to navigate an unbalanced organizational culture. Instead, you can try a new behavior that is more in line with your desired work–life preferences—you can conduct an experiment—and see if the organizational culture can handle your new behavior. In the process, the organizational culture might also change. David, the young investment banker, chose to address his unbalanced organizational culture by conducting just such an experiment.

David decided to gather some history on his observation that no one ever left the office before the managing director. Over a dinner break with a few colleagues who had worked at the Firm longer than he had, David asked how and when this unwritten policy of not leaving the office before the managing director developed. Everyone agreed that it was "just that way" and no one had ever questioned it. David sought his friends' assistance with an experiment. He decided to leave at 8:30 p.m. the next night (instead of his usual 10 or 11 p.m. departure)—after all of his work in preparation for the next day was completed. He asked his friends to observe what happened. The next morning, David's friends at work reported that no one, including the managing director, had even noticed when David had left the office. The group decided over the next few months to continue their experiment with one of them leaving before the managing director each week. Their work quality and quantity did not change. It appeared that they were slowly altering the unwritten rule of "face-time" without any consequence.

Instead of accepting the status quo and making assumptions that the culture was unchangeable, David experimented with a new way of doing things. Depending on your situation and comfort level, you may find yourself trying David's solution—to engage colleagues, without enlisting support from the higher levels of the organization, and challenge the organizational culture through experimentation. You may wish to consider this option if you have other colleagues that are willing to assist, experiment, and support you as you test new ways of working within the current organizational culture.

Also note that you can conduct an experiment on your own, without the help of others, and that this technique can work as well within nonwork settings as it does at work. For example, if you belong to an outdoors club and always find yourself offering to organize the quarterly camping trips, experiment with what happens if you do not say anything when trip planning comes up at the next event. Perhaps someone else will step up and offer to plan things. At home, are you tired of picking up all of your children's toys? If you leave them be for a few days, will your children or your spouse get more involved in clean-up? Conducting an experiment is one way to try on a desired behavior more in line with your work–life preferences and to see whether the organization is willing to accept or "absorb" that behavior.

Rewrite the Rules to Create a New Organizational Culture

As an alternative to experimenting with a new behavior, you can also make an explicit attempt to rewrite the "rules" of the organizational culture so that they are more supportive of work–life balance. Instead of behaving differently and hoping this behavior will change the culture, you can do the reverse—change the rules of the culture to make it easier for you to behave differently—in line with your work–life preferences. That was the approach taken by Lisa, the business owner and mother, to address the issues of unbalanced organizational culture in her life.

> After some reflection, Lisa realized that her family life represented the unbalanced organizational culture with which she was struggling. Although she and her husband both had full-time jobs, she was doing the majority of house and family upkeep on the weekends and always worried about how to maintain home operations and work responsibilities when something unexpected arose. After a long, nondefensive, and productive discussion with her husband, Lisa and he came up with a three-part approach: Lisa would have two hours each weekend that were completely her own without any responsibilities, each child would take on two additional chores, and Lisa's husband helped craft a "family crisis plan" that addressed possible solutions for the many scenarios that were causing Lisa to constantly worry. In addition, Lisa's husband committed to being more flexible and available for additional responsibilities and support.

On the basis of your particular situation and circumstances, you might try Lisa's solution—to create a new culture by rewriting the rules. In this scenario, you work to design something different that works and ask others to join in. You can experiment with this situation with your family; or, in a work scenario, you can use this when you are in a leadership position. You can engage your staff or team to work together to support the entire group in devising a more amenable work structure to support greater balance.

Although it can be more difficult to rewrite the rules of the culture when you are not in a leadership position, this can also be possible in organizations that are open to feedback from participants and employees. If you find yourself in this kind of culture but not in a decision-making role, you might also be able to use the rewrite-the-rules technique for navigating unbalanced organizational culture. For example, you might talk to the leader of the group or organization, speak to someone in HR about your concerns, talk to your boss, or start a discussion at a group meeting.

Set an Ultimatum and Be Comfortable With Possible Consequences

Lastly, you can navigate organizational culture by setting an ultimatum that is in line with your desired balance preferences and see if you can effect change in this way. Let's look at Graham, the bicycle industry professional and marketing association president, and see how he used the ultimatum technique to deal with the unbalanced organizational culture of the association.

> Graham had reached the end of his rope with his extensive service to his professional organization. This volunteer role was now impacting other areas of his life in ways that he was no longer willing to allow. With his new awareness that he could

not continue with this level of commitment, Graham notified the other board members of his time limits and of what he believed each of them needed to contribute to keep the organization operating at its current capacity. Graham communicated what he was willing to continue doing and had a few direct conversations with the board as a whole and with some individuals. He felt comfortable that he was doing all he could and that if others did not step up to their responsibilities, the association might need to reconsider how it was going to operate with a volunteer board.

If you discover an unbalanced organizational culture in situations in which you have a substantial degree of freedom and control, for example, as a volunteer in a professional or community organization, you might try Graham's solution—to set an ultimatum and be comfortable with the possible consequences. The ideal positive consequences of this situation is that other members of the organization will step up and take on additional responsibilities in order to lessen your load. The less-than-ideal consequences would be that you do not get the support you need to continue and that the organization cannot sustain itself without your level of work. In this case, this might mean that your decision would impact the viability of the organization. Clarity with your boundaries will be really important so you can make the right choice for yourself and not feel responsible or guilty for potential consequences.

The previous examples show a wide variety of possibilities in how you might choose to raise concerns with and/or address an unbalanced organizational culture. In addition, note that

Can Navigating Unbalanced Organizational Culture Cause Trouble?

It is important to note that whichever technique you use to navigate unbalanced organizational culture—leaving the organization, conducting an experiment, rewriting the rules of the organization, or setting an ultimatum—there could be negative consequences. Going against proscribed ways of operating could lead to negative outcomes. Choosing to leave an organization can also have a series of significant impacts on your life, your family, and/or your community. Thus, it is important for you to gauge possible risk and make decisions that feel comfortable to you.

you also have the option of choosing the status quo—that is, choosing to accept an unbalanced organizational culture and its undesirable impacts on your life. Choosing the status quo will likely not move you closer to your desired work–life balance, but that is fine if you are making a deliberate choice because you feel the trade–off of giving up some balance is worth the things you gain by staying with the status quo. If you do choose this approach, remember to schedule a check-in for yourself in the future to assess whether you would like to continue to accept the status quo or whether you would like to choose a new way of dealing with the unbalanced organizational culture.

Now it is your turn to consider which technique or techniques you would like to use to navigate the organizations in your life that have an unbalanced culture.

Define Organizational Possibilities: Now that you have seen the multiple ways that people can address unbalanced organizational culture, you are in a good position to start thinking about the ways in which you might want to address the issues of unbalanced organizational culture you have identified in your own life. Take out your *7 Keys Workbook and Journal* or other dedicated work space and spend some time reviewing the organizational challenges you identified earlier in the chapter (see the *Evaluate Your Organizations* fieldwork) and then begin defining possible options for addressing these issues. Think creatively as well as specifically. In the process, the following two questions may be helpful.

- What possibilities are there for addressing the organizational challenges to my desired work–life balance?

- How might I propose new ways of operating in and with my organization?

For example, if you identified that one component of your company's unbalanced culture is that everyone seems to answer emails very late into the evening and extremely early in the morning, you might brainstorm the following three possibilities or new ways for addressing the issue to allow for more balance in your own life:

- talk to your boss and tell her your concerns about what seems to be the norm of answering emails at all hours of the day and night

- talk to a few peers and see if they have the same concern and come up with a plan to change the way everyone seems to pride themselves in answering emails at 1 a.m.

- stop answering emails after 8 p.m. or before 7 a.m. and see what, if anything, happens, or if anyone even cares or notices.

After you have generated a list of possible solutions for navigating the unbalanced organizational culture in question, decide which solution you would like to try first. When you are making your choice, you might consider which option feels the least risky, scary, or worrisome. You might also contemplate which solution fits with your style and feels the most comfortable to you. Once you decide on the solution, circle it. A little later in the chapter, you are going to take the solution you selected and break it into manageable steps that you can enact over time. But first, let's examine some of the challenges you may face as you contemplate putting one of these solutions into action.

Now that you have brainstormed possible solutions for navigating the unbalanced organizational culture in question and decided which solution you would like to implement first, how do you feel? Are you excited? Nervous? Fearful? Wary? If you find yourself feeling uncomfortable at the thought of implementing your chosen solution, consider the other solutions available to you and see if any of those feel better. If not, you might also consider the challenges that make it hard for many of us to actively navigate unbalanced organizational culture. These challenges are described in the following text.

Challenges to Addressing Unbalanced Organizational Culture

Even with increased awareness of the change you desire within your organization and insight into which approach you would ideally like to use to effect this change, making changes within your organizations can be a very difficult path to walk. There are a variety of reasons why people do not attempt to address an unbalanced organizational culture. These reasons include those that follow.

Fear for Job Security

You encounter this challenge when you fear that if you speak up, doing so may negatively impact your job security. You may worry that you will be seen as a "complainer," that you might not be perceived as loyal to the company, and that the organization will want to replace you as a result. In most cases, addressing a concern will give you insight into whether the decision makers within the organization are open to helping or collaborating. If you get a negative response when you raise your concern, you then have the choice of what you want to do next. Of course, you cannot predict the future and your fears could be realized. You have to decide what you are comfortable in addressing.

Creates More Work

You encounter this challenge when you fear that requesting a change may actually require more work for yourself. If you bring a problem and a solution to a leader's attention, you may get asked to be part of a large solution that requires additional time, energy, and commitment that you do not have. This very well might be the case. Ideally, if you are bringing up a concern, mentioning an accompanying solution will allow you to be seen as a proactive problem solver, which is always a good thing. You need to evaluate if investing in the solution is worth it to you.

Might Have to Quit

You encounter this challenge when you fear that if you ask for something that is very important to you and it is not respected, you may feel compelled to look for another job out of integrity (this is a values issue). You may not be willing to take this risk. If you feel strongly that not addressing your concerns is an affront to your integrity and values and you choose to take a stand, be prepared for the possibility that a negative response from the organization might increase your motivation to leave the organization. Of course, if you do not get the desired results, you may still choose to stay at your current job because you believe it gives you more than leaving and making a point.

Not a Team Player

You encounter this challenge when you fear that your colleagues may develop a negative impression of you after you ask for organizational changes. They may no longer see you as a team player and may believe that you do not want to work as hard as they do. Of course, this may be the case, but often peers will see you as someone who is addressing a valid concern and will respect you for doing so. Ideally, if you go to a boss or Human Resources to bring up this (or any issue), it will also be kept confidential.

Commitment in Question

In relation to community or volunteer organizations, you may fear that peers, friends, or those in need of your support will question your commitment to "the cause." This fear may actually come true. Thus, you need to weigh the importance of your desire for a more manageable work–life balance and the possible repercussions of being seen as someone who is uncommitted or even "selfish."

Emotional Discomfort

You may fear the emotional repercussions that get created in your family as a result of making a change. For families, raising these issues may require an entire overhaul of family roles that could lead to anger, discomfort, resistance, or outright hostility for expressing dissatisfaction with how the family has operated in the past. With any significant change, some parties involved may not be happy with the results. If you choose to address the imbalances in your family culture, you can also acknowledge that it may be difficult and highlight the positive outcomes once everyone gets comfortable with the new normal.

Note: The previous challenges are all related to various fears that may prevent people from acting to address a concern within an organization of which they are a part. With any fear, it could be based in reality. In other words, the results you do not want *could* happen. Often, though, the thought of the fear coming to fruition ("oh my, what if I lose my job if I ask for more balance?") is more debilitating than actually taking the plunge, bringing up an important issue just because it is important to you, and facing whatever consequence may arise—positive or negative. Many people forget their significant store of resilience to overcome fear and take more control in making change.

So, with all of these possible downsides, why would anyone try to make changes to an unbalanced organizational culture? You will decide to make a change to overcome this barrier to work–life balance when the discomfort from not doing so is more uncomfortable than keeping the status quo. Making changes when you are impacted by unbalanced organizational culture requires fortitude, courage, and willingness to take a risk. It also helps if you can find an advocate within your organization to provide support, guidance, and encouragement. You also need to be patient with yourself and the process if you decide to forge ahead and address this barrier. Your journey may be met with resistance and may only advance via baby steps. You have to decide on what terms and in what capacity you want to overcome this barrier and to be aware that there may be consequences outside of your control and influence.

Now that you have reviewed the possible challenges to navigating work–life balance, take some time to contemplate whether any apply to you. If so, what do you need to do to work through this particular challenge (or challenges)?

When you are ready to move beyond the challenges you face in navigating unbalanced organizational culture, the next field-work exercise will help you create a tangible plan, with small action steps, for actively navigating the unbalanced organizational culture you have identified earlier in the chapter.

Take a First Step to Address an Unbalanced Organizational Culture: Earlier in the chapter, you selected which solution you would like to implement when navigating your unbalanced organizational culture. To make the process of implementing this solution more manageable, I recommend that you break down this solution into a plan with very small steps.

First, return to the solution you selected in the previous fieldwork (*Define Organizational Possibilities*). Then, over the next week, choose a first action step to take to implement the solution you identified in the previous fieldwork. This may range from setting up a conversation with a sympathetic peer or supervisor to getting an alternative perspective of your concern or starting to gather feedback from colleagues to see if others experience your same concerns. Or, you might decide to take a big leap and sit down with your boss and "put it all out there."

Regardless of what you choose to do, the important part of using this key is taking a first step, gauging the result and how you feel about it, and continuing ahead or choosing to stop. So, now it is time to define your first step. When you are ready, take out your *7 Keys Workbook and Journal* or other dedicated work space and write down answers that correspond to the following bullet points.

- I will take the following step ….
- My desired outcome of this step is ….
- The support I need to take this step is ….

For example, you might write …

- *I will take the following step – Talk to my boss about my concerns regarding the organizational cultural norm of answering emails very late into the night.*
- *My desired outcome of this step – To let my boss know that I am very committed to my work and the company, and to get her "buy-in" that I'm not going to respond to work emails at very late hours.*
- *The support I need to take this step – A discussion with a peer at work to make sure that he thinks I am not asking too much; and a reminder from my husband that my increased stress about this is not good for my health or our family.*

After you have responded to the previous bullet points and taken the first step, answer the following questions.

- How did I feel taking this step?
- What did I learn from this step?

If you are satisfied with this first step and want to attempt further change, then start the process over again, defining the next step needed to implement your plan. You may still be working your way through making adjustments to one particular organization or you may be ready to move on to addressing a different organizational challenge altogether. Either way, remember that any time you wish to stop, for whatever reason, you get to choose to stop the process. As with all of the keys, you need to find a way to put them into practice on your terms!

◆ ◆ ◆

In sum, there a variety of techniques for navigating unbalanced organizational culture, from experimenting with new behavior to rewriting the rules of the organization to setting an ultimatum, or even leaving the organization altogether. Which solution you decide to implement will depend on the organization, as well as your personal style, preferences, and comfort level. Whichever solutions you ultimately implement, you will be taking proactive steps and making deliberate choices reflective of you and the life you want to lead.

- Unbalanced organizational culture means that structures, policies, expectations, and/or history of the organization do not support creating an environment in which work–life balance is a concern, priority, or even a possibility.
- Organizations with unbalanced culture can include your family, volunteer organizations, professional associations, religious institutions, and your employer.
- Pay attention to how each of the organizations with which you are involved impact your work–life balance preferences.
- Before addressing unbalanced organizational culture, determine whether the situation is temporary or permanent, situational or ongoing, and whether or not it is acceptable to speak up within the organization.
- Know your time limits regarding how you want to interact with your organization(s).
- Partner with family members to alter an unbalanced organizational culture at home.
- Addressing unbalanced organizational culture at work can be daunting. Find an advocate and/or get support from colleagues, supervisors, and/or leaders within the organization.
- The concept of "Fire Your Boss" means you have taken a mental leap regarding your current situation and you have nothing to lose by asking for exactly what you want. This is a last ditch effort where you no longer worry about the

consequences of taking action regarding the unbalanced organizational culture.

- Challenges to addressing an unbalanced organizational culture include fear for job security, fear it may create more work for you, fear that you might have to quit, fear that you might not be perceived as a team player, fear that your commitment may be questioned, and/or fear that you may experience emotional discomfort.

- For this challenging barrier, you are most likely to make a change when the pain from not doing anything outweighs the risk, possible discomfort, or pain from attempting to do something to improve the situation.

KEY 7

Engage in Self-Care

How would you choose to spend the day if the powers-that-be in your life said to you, "Today is a day off. Take the day and do whatever you'd like with it—as long as you spend it in a way that rejuvenates you. No errands, no chores, no work allowed"? Would you go for a long and lazy bike ride? Would you tuck yourself onto the couch with a book and a cup of hot tea? Would you take your boat or your motorcycle or your antique car out for a spin? Would you go to the spa and get a massage? Would you head over to the community garden and tend your plot? Or maybe you would call a friend to meet for lunch, go to the gym, or spend the afternoon drawing with charcoal? How would you choose to spend a day that was only about taking care of you?

There are few things more enjoyable in life than giving yourself the gift of rejuvenation, what I call *self-care*. Perhaps this is because most of us take care of ourselves so infrequently and because we live in such a busy world, one that often places continual demands on our time. Perhaps this is because we live in a culture where the norm is to work many hours each week, such that there is hardly any time left over at the end of the day to care for ourselves. Perhaps this is because we feel guilty taking care of ourselves, like it is irresponsible or indulgent. Whatever the reason, many of us struggle to make time to take care of ourselves throughout the day, the week, and the year. Taking care of ourselves often feels like a guilty pleasure or an unusual luxury.

Think about it. How did you feel when you read the first paragraph of this chapter? Did your heart start beating a little faster at the vision of spending a day exactly as you wanted—with no work allowed? Maybe you felt excited, maybe you felt nervous, or maybe you felt disdainful, thinking—"no way, not me, successful people don't take time off!" Maybe you thought, "Me, take a day off? If only I should be so lucky!" Whatever your reaction, I suspect your response to the idea of taking a day just for yourself was strong, whether marked by enthusiasm, disbelief, or disapproval.

As you will discover in this chapter, the last of the keys to work–life balance described in this book is *engaging in self-care*. Many people who struggle on the path to work–life balance do so because they are missing this essential key —they do not make time for self-care and they may not even realize its value. In such cases, *lack of self-care* becomes a barrier to work–life balance. People in such cases are neglecting an important component of themselves *outside of their work realm*; in the process, they are also steering their work–life balance off of its preferred route. In addition, this lack of self-care can in turn affect their ability to be at their best when *at work*.

In sum, lack of self-care diminishes both the work and life components of the work–life mix. In contrast, taking time to care for yourself is likely to enhance your sense of satisfaction with your work–life mix as well as to help you be at your best both at work and in your life in general.

Developing Awareness of the Key

A Closer Look at the Concept

Self-care refers to making choices and taking action in order to increase your physical, mental, emotional, spiritual, and/or social well-being. Self-care is all about you— choosing to do what you want to enhance your energy, happiness, ability to relax, health, attitude … whatever rejuvenates, refreshes, reinvigorates, or relaxes you. The choices involved with self-care are completely subjective and based on what you desire for yourself. Here are some examples of self-care.

drawing a picture

reading a book

taking a nap

watching a movie

getting a manicure or pedicure

eating a healthy snack or meal

going for a swim

going for a run

riding your bike

playing sports

painting

working out

spending an afternoon doing photography

playing an instrument

meeting a friend

calling a family member

going for a hike

taking a warm bath

drinking a cup of hot tea

visiting your favorite coffee shop

going to place of worship

meditating

doing yoga

writing a letter

buying flowers

cooking a special meal

window shopping

planning an adventure

roaming in a gallery

reading the Sunday newspaper uninterrupted

This list is just a starting point regarding the different ways you might choose to take care of yourself. In truth, there are many ways you can take care of yourself, and, as I mentioned earlier, what constitutes self-care is different for each of us. For example, some people find going for a run to be incredibly relaxing (serving as self-care), while others would rather walk barefoot across a board of nails (not serving as self-care)! While one person gets reenergized by reading a book or engaging in some other solitary activity, another might generate the most energy by connecting with other people—through a phone call or a lunch date, for example. There are no "shoulds" regarding self-care … this key is personal and relates to whatever helps you feel good.

Let's look at Amy, the vice president of business development for a national retail chain store, to see how lack of self-care can contribute to a person's sense of dissatisfaction with work–life balance.

> Now a single parent of two college-aged kids, Amy had worked her entire professional life to provide for her children and give them what they now have—a fortunate childhood and a good college education. After reaching this accomplishment and returning each night to her empty house, though, she is realizing that she has no hobbies, interests, or even many friends outside of work. Her years of not taking care of her personal self—the woman who operates outside of her profession—have caught up with her. She does not know how to fill her free time when she is at home, and when she is at work, she has lost her zest and her drive. As a result, Amy is not happy with her home life or her work life. Although she is a trusted advisor and confidante of the CEO at her company and is very well respected by her work peers and direct reports, Amy has been noticing over the past few months that she is no longer

motivated at work. The projects that she once enjoyed managing no longer feel interesting or exciting. She used to relish arriving at work early to enjoy the quiet and her enhanced productivity, and she liked to stay late to make sure all of her projects were progressing as planned. She lived and breathed work, and she thought that was all she wanted and needed. Yet, now she is exhausted and often has pain in her neck and back. She has not only lost motivation for work, it seems as if she has little motivation for anything.

Amy represents someone who has lacked self-care for many years. Only now, though, after her children have moved out of the house does she feel the consequences of this lack of self-care deeply. As long as she was motivated to succeed at work in order to provide well for her children, she was able to largely ignore her own interests and needs outside of work. But with the goal of providing for her children mostly met and an empty house in the evenings and on weekends, all the space in Amy's life makes her realize the need to care for herself. Her life feels lopsided, with too much energy spent at work and not enough energy dedicated to her life outside of work. As a result, Amy is dissatisfied with her work–life balance, even if she is not sure how exactly to change her life.

As was the case for Amy, the constant act of doing for others, whether professionally or personally, can drain your energy. If you do not have a mechanism to refuel—to regain this lost energy—you are unlikely to move toward your desired work–life balance, as your "vehicle" (your body and mind) will not support you on your journey.

Think of it this way. If your journey involves a car, you want to make sure that your car is well maintained. You would not head on a cross-country drive (or maybe not even on a long day trip) without checking your oil and tire pressure, filling up your windshield wiper fluid and filling up your gas tank. When you have low tire pressure, your gas mileage goes down; if your oil runs out, you risk an engine seizure; and the last thing you want is an empty tank of gas or other car problem to interrupt your travels. Preventative maintenance is critical to a smooth-running vehicle and safe travels. Similarly, self-care is essential to full engagement and satisfaction with personal and professional endeavors.

The Importance of Self-Care

When you have a busy life, taking the time to care for yourself may seem like a luxury you cannot afford. In fact, if you want more time to invest in cultivating your desired work–life balance, it might even seem counterintuitive to spend time on something as seemingly frivolous as self-care. For example, maybe you have decided that you would like to cultivate more family time. Since your time is precious, you might be thinking, "I can't add self-care to my routine—as it is, I barely have time outside of work for my family. If I take time to care for myself, I won't have anything left to give to my family."

Admittedly, it will be easier to find time for self-care in some stages of your life than others (e.g., when kids are older, when you are not balancing work and school, or when work deadlines are not crazy). Nonetheless, even when times are stressful and tight, self-care can play an important role in helping you manage the stress and hang on to some sense of balance and sanity. This is not to say that you need to take every Friday off to go to the spa or on a day hike, but caring for yourself on a regular basis—even in little ways—is essential to your health, well-being, and work–life satisfaction. In fact, you might even need self-care more than ever during those times of your life that are particularly intense, such as after the birth of a new baby or when a large work deadline looms. It can be the little moments of self-care that help you maintain some semblance of stability in your life when chaos is swirling around you.

The reality is that we need to invest time in *ourselves* in order to operate at full efficiency. So often, when we are very busy, we let go of the things that are most rejuvenating and energizing to us in order to *do* more. We believe we are making the right choices as we are checking more items off of our to-do lists, without realizing the consequences to our work–life satisfaction, including our sense of productivity at work and our contentment outside of our jobs. We assume that we can become more successful at work by skipping routines of caring for ourselves, when, in fact, it is often the opposite. Yes, leaving self-care out temporarily may help us meet deadlines or increase output, in the short-term, but an absence of self-care in our lives over the long-term often has detrimental effects—whether on our health, emotions, motivation, efficiency, creativity, or productivity. Let's look at the case of Jaclyn, a busy entrepreneur, mother, active community member, friend, wife, and amateur musician.

Jaclyn works at home, which allows her to be involved in her five-year-old son's school while putting in many hours building her business. She works during the day while her son is at school, takes a few hours off when he returns home, and often finds herself back in her office after her son is sleeping, until well past 11 p.m. or midnight most weeknights. Over the past year, her business has been growing. Although she is excited and proud of the results, she notices she is no longer practicing her flute or taking breaks for exercise and is having to say no to friends and community activities with which she would like to be involved. To add to this, her son has begun waking up most nights causing a few hours of sleep loss each night. Before the sleep interruptions, she felt she could hold it all together. Now, with three weeks of less than five hours of sleep each night, she has reached her limit. She is tired, cranky, scattered, and inefficient. She feels like a different person and is questioning her ability to successfully maintain what has always been important to her—her business, her music, her community, and her meaningful time with her family.

Unlike Amy, who had not engaged in self-care for years, Jaclyn generally had a good routine of self-care, involving exercise, music practice, and community participation. Yet, when work got busy and her family life started demanding a bit more (i.e., her increased business and son's sleep problems), Jaclyn let her self-care routine slip.

This is a common response, right? For most of us, self-care is the first activity to "go" when we have to trim our schedules down to make way for increased responsibilities. Again, in the short-term, this can be an acceptable way to handle deadlines, life challenges, and emergencies. Over the long-term, though, ignoring self-care can have the opposite of its intended effect. Instead of making us more productive, skipping self-care can leave us feeling drained—or, like Jaclyn, tired, cranky, scattered, and inefficient. By eliminating self-care, we eventually become less productive and efficient, instead of more so.

Another important point to consider is that caring for yourself often needs to come before caring for others. It is much like the advice that flight attendants give when reviewing safety information as a flight is taking off: They always tell you that you need to put your own safety mask on first in case of emergency, rather than helping someone who is with you. In this case, you cannot take care of anyone else, even the child next to you, if you are not breathing and well. The same is often true at work and in life. You can only be truly helpful to others when you are in a "well-maintained" state.

Ultimately, taking good care of yourself gives you more energy, increases your focus and productivity, keeps you in a better mood, and allows you to sleep better. It also creates a positive feedback loop. When you nurture yourself, you feel better and usually have a more positive outlook on your life. This pattern then continues—in which feeling better about your life leads to continued self-care.

Identifying the Barrier: Lack of Self-Care

If you find it challenging to engage in self-care, then you are facing the barrier of *lack of self-care*. You can overcome this particular barrier by defining your self-care gaps and then making choices for greater self-care.

Here are some examples of lack of self-care:

- inefficient sleep
- inefficient exercise
- unhealthy diet or unhealthy snacking for energy
- too much caffeine
- smoking
- no "downtime"
- no hobbies or nonwork interests
- no *real* vacation.

Do any of the previous items sound familiar? Have you already started to add some of your own lack of self-care items to the list? The following exercise will help you identify the areas in your life where you are currently lacking self-care.

Where Are You Lacking? Now it is your turn to identify any areas where you are experiencing lack of self-care. Look back over the past week and review how you spent your time, what choices you made, and which choices you *did not* make—vis à vis self-care. You will be describing ways in which self-care took a backseat in your life and work.

Since you are identifying a *lack* of something—something that does not currently exist in your life—it might be tricky at first to complete this exercise. It is often easier to spot something that exists than to identify something that does not. If you find this exercise to be challenging for this reason, you might find it helpful to use the previous bulleted list as you reflect on the ways in which you might currently lack self-care. Are you lacking sleep? Are you eating poorly or skipping meals? Are you overworking yourself, whether at the office or at home? Is your time each week devoid of any hobbies? Another way to help identify areas where you currently lack self-care is to think about the things for which you long during stressful times. For what do you yearn in these cases (A nap? A night out with your friends? A trip to the movie theater? A vacation to the islands?) If you filled in the blank of "If only I had more time, I would _____," what would you say?

Examples of how Jaclyn (one of our earlier examples) completed these fieldwork exercises are included here.

Ways in which I didn't take care of myself last week:

	Date	Description
1.	Monday	stayed in office until 10 p.m. finishing report
2.	Monday	didn't eat during day, too busy
3.	Wednesday	skipped flute lesson
4.	Thursday	didn't schedule very overdue doctor appointment

As you can see, Jaclyn skipped self-care in a number of places in the previous week.

When you are ready, take out your *7 Keys Workbook and Journal* or other dedicated work space and record the ways in which you did not take care of yourself in the previous week.

Once you have identified the areas in your life where you are currently lacking self-care, I encourage you to take the exercise a step further by considering the impact that this lack of self-care has had on your life. Before you can make any adjustments in the way you take care of yourself, it is important to understand the impact of your current behaviors. For example, if the impact is not that significant, it may not be worth investing time and energy in making a change.

 Impact of Current Self-Care Choices: For each item in the list you just generated regarding areas where self-care was lacking in your life (see *Where Are You Lacking?* fieldwork), describe how that missed opportunity for self-care (that choice) impacted you and/or how it made you feel. Here is an excerpt of Jaclyn's responses to this fieldwork. These answers correspond to the areas of self-care that she identified as lacking in the previous fieldwork exercise.

How my choices impacted me.

1. *exhausted the next day, short with my son and husband, wiped out*
2. *initial feeling of productivity but energy crash in afternoon, overate at dinner*

3. *disappointed and angry*
4. *annoyed, feeling that I'm not walking my talk as health is very important to me*

As you can see, seemingly simple choices led Jaclyn to experience all kinds of undesirable consequences and feelings.

Now, it is your turn again. When you are ready, review the list you completed in the previous *Where Are You Lacking?* fieldwork exercise regarding lack of self-care and write in your *7 Keys Workbook and Journal* or other dedicated work space a corresponding impact for each choice to not engage in self-care.

Now that you have written this list, take some time to read it over. How do you feel overall about the state of your self-care activities? Write your answer down in your journal. If it is helpful, you may also want to address the larger question of what you have discovered from completing this exercise.

◆ ◆ ◆

While in the process of identifying a lack of self-care in your life—and related impacts—a wide variety of feelings may emerge, including (but not limited to) anger, frustration, disappointment, sadness, surprise (either that self-care is so little, or that you did not even miss it), greater understanding, and compassion for yourself ("no wonder I do not feel energized, I never take time for anything that matters to me.") Happily, most people conducting this exercise also experience increased motivation to engage in self-care in the future. Although it can be sad, frustrating, or disappointing to come to terms with the many ways you have *not* taken care of yourself in the past, it can also be very exciting and motivating to realize that you can make changes in the future. Starting to engage in self-care can also be easy and fun.

Putting the Key Into Practice

Engaging in self-care is possible! It requires a commitment of time and energy, a willingness to put yourself first at times, a level of clarity on what is most meaningful and energizing to you, and an environment of support. When these four criteria are present, self-care is less likely to be pushed aside for something else. Paying attention to these factors means that you have cleared space, both physically and emotionally, to do what is "care-full" for yourself; you have decided to say "no" to other competing demands on your time, for the short time you have dedicated to self-care; you know what type of care will be meaningful to you, regardless of what other people think; and you have friends, family, and other advocates encouraging you and assisting in giving you what you need in order to do what you have decided is important to your care and well-being.

Let's look at what is needed for self-care in more detail.

Commit Time and Energy

This means putting aside specific, sacred time that is reserved just for you and your desired self-care practice or activity. Just as you schedule time for work meetings, training programs, volunteer commitments, doctor appointments, haircuts, and other work and personal commitments, you need to schedule time for self-care. Self-care does not magically happen—you need to put it on your calendar by blocking out time for it. Just as your calendar, PDA, or assistant remind you where you need to be and when for work commitments, use these same resources to remind you it is time to engage in self-care. Then, follow through on the appointments! It can be tempting to cancel scheduled self-care because you are not accountable to anyone else or will not be letting anyone else down when you skip self-care. Yet, remembering how good you feel after self-care can help you stick to your appointments. And the more you engage in self-care, the more you tend to keep engaging in self-care—it feels pleasant, so you continue with it.

Here is another tip that might be helpful in this process of committing time and energy to self-care. In Jim Loehr and Tony Schwartz's *The Power of Full Engagement*, the authors talk about creating "rituals" in order to make sure important things happen. A first step to a ritual is doing it regularly. If you schedule a workout, a music lesson, a massage, or a nap in your calendar, it is much more likely to happen. If you do this regularly, eventually it will become a ritual or habit—something that has now become part of how you effectively operate. Think about the first step you can take in making a ritual for yourself and your own self-care.

Put Yourself First, at Times

After you have blocked out the actual time for self-care, you need to be mentally and emotionally comfortable with it. You need to believe that it is okay to do something for just you, even in the midst of a busy, demanding work and personal schedule. Going for a walk in the woods or meeting a friend for a drink will not be pleasurable or rejuvenating if you feel you are stealing time from others during your reserved time.

To get the most out of your scheduled self-care (and to follow through on your appointments for self-care), you need to make an internal shift (a sort of values change) toward believing that there is a benefit from focusing on yourself for a few small chunks of time each week. Since the external demands for your time are unlikely to change immediately, it is only by making an internal shift of values that you will find the strength and commitment to follow through on your scheduled self-care. How do you need to mentally reframe the idea of giving time to yourself? What makes it feel right for you, and also right for others that you care for, to create a small oasis of self-care time?

Stay Clear on What Matters to You

The way you apply self-care in your life is a very personal process. What may look like self-care to someone else may be absolute misery to you. Thus, you will want to make sure the self-care you schedule for yourself is really about you, not about what others recommend for you. Here is an example.

> Renee, an insurance company executive, has been asked time and again by her friends to go on an annual "girls' weekend" to get away from the busy demands of work and personal life. At times, Renee has felt pressured to go along because weekends away without work, husband, children, or cooking and weekends full of fun, laughing, and "downtime" with friends are "supposed to be" good for her as her friends so strongly believe. After giving it a long thought, though, Renee realizes that real self-care to her is having the freedom and flexibility to do whatever she wants without having to come to a group consensus on what movie to watch, where to eat, what time to go for a walk, or when to leave and arrive anywhere. Renee's ideal re-energizing weekend away would

be alone, at a hotel, with a good book, where she could order room service when she wants, sleep and wake when she wants, and not have to alter her schedule for anyone. It is not that she does not love being with her friends. She has simply realized that if she is going to invest a very valuable weekend in getting away and taking care of herself, she wants it to be exactly what she wants most.

Like Renee, before you act on your self-care plan, make sure it is what you really want for yourself. Quiet the "shoulds" that self-care is supposed to be like something that someone else imagines for them or for you. What are your self-care priorities? How do you want to feel when you are taking care of just yourself?

Surround Yourself With a Supportive Environment

With three of the four pieces of the self-care puzzle in place, the last part is making sure that people around you support you in making this process happen. Whether you are putting aside a few minutes each day, an hour a week, and/or a day a month for your self-care priorities, determine a few people who can offer support and encouragement in developing and continuing self-care practices that work for you. This may mean finding a partner with whom to exercise, a reliable babysitter for nights out with your partner or spouse, a boss who understands the importance of "downtime," and your family members (children included) knowing when and how to respect and honor the self-care time you have carefully carved out of your busy day, week, month, and year. Who can you seek out to be your advocate, ally, supporter, or teammate?

Okay, you acknowledge the value of self-care … now what? Next comes the fun part of the self-care process: selecting meaningful ways to take care of *you*!

Designing Your Self-Care Prescription Plan: Now the fun begins! It is time to clarify what type of self-care activities are meaningful to you. These are the things that you imagine on your most busy, stressful, overwhelming days—the thoughts that you have when you think, "If only I could do [fill-in-the-blank]," things would be better, more meaningful, bearable, or fun.

Take out your *7 Keys Workbook and Journal* or other dedicated work space and start by writing down ten things you can do daily or weekly to engage in self-care. They can be big, like an hour a day at the gym, or smaller ... like picking up fresh flowers once a week. Just make sure that each item energizes you, makes you feel good, or relaxes you. You do not need to do any of these now, just define them.

Amy, who previously lacked insight into how she wanted to fill her free time outside of work, wrote the following list.

Ten daily and/or weekly activities, choices, or lack-of-activities that will enhance my self-care.

1. *buy artwork to brighten up home*
2. *find a gentle exercise class that is close to the office*
3. *create a profile on dating website*
4. *pack a healthy lunch 2x week*
5. *reconnect with old college friend*
6. *load music on MP3 player that has been collecting dust for a year*
7. *volunteer at the animal shelter*
8. *set my alarm clock a half hour later on workdays*
9. *visit art museum this weekend/get membership*
10. *spend time on hammock.*

As you are writing up your list, feel free to borrow from the list of self-care activities shown at the start of the chapter or to review it for inspiration. You might also find it helpful to interview your friends regarding the kinds of things they do to care for themselves. You can also think back to how you spent your free time when you were a child and had less life responsibilities or even to how you have taken care of yourself in the past during less busy or stressful times.

Once you have identified your shorter-term self-care activities, I recommend that you move on to defining longer-term self-care activities—those that occur either on a monthly or annual basis. This might mean a monthly massage or night-out with friends, or an annual vacation to a meaningful location. When thinking and writing down your choices, turn off your internal editor, the voice that may say, "you can't do that!" and try to have fun with the exercise. You need to quiet the voice that makes it easy to say "no" to self-care and turn up the volume on the support for this process. By doing so, you can increase the likelihood of making self-care a priority.

For another example, here is Amy's list of long-term self-care activities.

Five monthly or yearly activities, choices, or lack-of-activities that will enhance my self-care.

1. *plan a vacation to Ireland*
2. *start a monthly book group*
3. *turn spare room into craft area*
4. *calligraphy lessons*
5. *invite neighbors over for dinner party every few months*

◆　◆　◆

Once you are done creating these two self-care lists (short-term and long-term), I recommend that you take some time to review these lists. How do you feel when reviewing them? Hopefully, your feelings include excitement, desire, anticipation, and motivation.

If your response includes negative emotions, such as nervousness or fear, that is perfectly natural. Since your most recent way of operating has been to avoid self-care, it may take some time to get comfortable with your new self-care routine. There have probably been reasons until now—in the form of beliefs or excuses—that have stopped you from engaging in self-care.

Let's look at some of the common beliefs or excuses that might get in the way of putting your self-care prescription plan into action.

- "A good parent is always available." (Belief)
- "I can't leave the office for 'fun' if I'm not completely caught up with my work." (Belief)
- "To get promoted, I must work 70 hours per week." (Belief)
- "It seems frivolous to do something just for me when I have so much to do at home." (Belief)
- "I can't go to the gym because it is too crowded during the times I could possibly get there." (Excuse)
- "I can't plan a weekend away because I never know when a big deal will close." (Excuse)
- "I shouldn't plan a vacation—what if I lose my job?" (Excuse)
- "It's been too long since I spoke with my old friends so why bother reaching out?" (Excuse)

These are just a handful of the many excuses or beliefs that might get in the way of your putting self-care into practice. You are likely to uncover many more. Thus, when you are ready, take some time to contemplate which excuses and beliefs have stopped you from engaging in self-care in the past or that you anticipate might challenge your efforts to enact your new self-care plan.

 Ensuring Successful Self-Care: Once you have defined what may hold you back from taking care of yourself, let's look at the benefits that will come from greater self-care. Quantifying the benefits you see in making these self-care choices may help you successfully incorporate these new behaviors into your life. When defining these benefits, imagine the impact your increased self-care will have on your energy, happiness, focus, relationships, sleep, health, and more. Come up with at least five benefits you will receive from your new behaviors. Amy generated the following list of benefits regarding her self-care plan.

Benefits of Greater Self-Care:

1. *enjoying time at home more (due to new artwork on walls)*
2. *looking forward to connecting with others outside of work*
3. *more meaning in life (due to work at animal shelter and engaging in hobbies/creativity)*
4. *feeling healthier and lessening pain in back/neck (due to better diet and exercise)*
5. *excited about my future (looking forward to vacation and dating)*

As you can see, the benefits that Amy defined have quite a significant and holistic influence on her well-being. These benefits impact many areas of her life—social, physical, emotional, and intellectual.

It is now time to implement your self-care plan. I recommend that you begin by choosing one or two of the daily/weekly items that you identified earlier (see the *Designing Your Self-Care Prescription Plan for* fieldwork)—ideally, one or two that feel easiest to incorporate into your day or week to set yourself up for early success. Then, schedule these items in some meaningful way—plan a date with a friend, or schedule a class, appointment, or meeting with yourself. In other words, move from thinking about it to actually doing it. If you find an excuse or a belief getting in the way of your self-care choices, revisit your list of benefits to support you in making a firmer choice and commitment toward self-care.

During this first week, pay attention to the benefits of keeping these dates and times for and with yourself. After the first week, expand to include another one or two daily/weekly choices and also start to plan one monthly or annual priority.

This process is about trying new behaviors, looking for ways to make them become a ritual, and quantifying the benefits for yourself in doing so. As you keep adding small quantities of self-care into your day and week, notice how it impacts other areas of your life. Pay attention to the results and be open to making changes that support the continuation of a self-care practice.

◆ ◆ ◆

In sum, good self-care supports you in moving toward your desired work–life balance. Stepping out of the busy-ness of your very full professional and personal life allows you more frequent opportunities to pause and evaluate what is most important to you. Having a full tank of fuel also supports you during more stressful periods. The better you feel about yourself, the more likely you will be able to make choices that move you toward your preferred future state for work–life balance.

POSTCARD *from the* road

- Self-care is about making choices and taking action in order to increase your physical, mental, emotional, spiritual, and/or social well-being.
- Self-care supports greater work–life balance by enhancing your energy, focus, productivity, mood, sleep, and more.
- Lack of self-care includes inefficient sleep, inefficient exercise, unhealthy eating and drinking, smoking, and no rest or relaxation. This list can be endless.
- The four steps toward self-care require a commitment of time and energy, putting yourself first at times, clarity on what matters to you, and a supportive environment.
- Self-care is not about "shoulds." There is no one right way to take care of yourself. You get to choose what enhances your life most.
- Plan your self-care options on a daily/weekly time frame as well as on a monthly and annual basis.
- Excuses and beliefs can get in the way of implementing self-care choices.
- Clearly defining the benefits of greater self-care will support the implementation of your self-care prescription plan.
- Get support in implementing your self-care from a partner, friend, or colleague who understands the importance of this investment.
- Pay attention to the positive feelings and residual benefits of your new self-care choices in order to maintain this commitment to yourself.

The Journey Continues: Taking Stock and Maintaining Momentum

Y ou have reached a significant landmark on your journey toward a more desired work–life balance. As with any long road trip, when you come upon a historic site, a must-see vista, or a roadside attraction, you often choose to stop. You may take time to enjoy the new location, stretch your legs, acknowledge how far you have come, re-evaluate the route ahead, and make sure you and your vehicle are ready for the rest of the trip. In this chapter, I encourage you to do the same regarding your own journey toward work–life balance.

Up to this point, your journey has involved delving into each of the 7 keys to work–life balance by learning about the way that each key works, the benefits of using each key, and techniques for putting each key into action. The journey has also involved examining the challenges related to using the keys— learning about the 7 barriers that can pop up on one's journey toward work–life balance and that often make it difficult to use that particular key to work–life balance. Through the fieldwork in each chapter, you have explored whether any of these barriers affect you and, if so, identified the specifics of how these barriers inhibit your own journey in work and life. In all likelihood, you have also taken a lot of action toward removing those barriers and using each key to move closer to your ideal work–life balance.

Given all the reflection and hard work in which you have engaged, this is a fitting time to pause and appreciate all that you have learned. This final chapter aims at helping you do that, by providing a review of your journey thus far and inviting you to reflect on where you are on that journey. Much of the chapter will serve as a review of the 7 keys used to cultivate work–life balance, with an opportunity to reflect on how you are currently putting each key into practice.

The 7 Keys

So as to reinforce all the tools you have gained by reading this book, let's begin by reviewing the 7 keys you can use on your journey toward greater work–life balance.

Develop Priorities

To review, a *priority* is a goal, task, or action that takes precedence over other goals, tasks, or actions. This particular key to work–life balance involves ...

1. being clear on your priorities
2. knowing how to implement your priorities
3. successfully maintaining your priorities in the face of challenges to them.

The first step—being clear on your priorities—begins with defining your personal and professional visions. Your vision is a description of all that you want to accomplish in your work and in the bigger picture of your life. A clear vision allows for easier decision-making regarding how you spend your valuable resource of time—that is, regarding which priorities you set for using your time.

The second step—implementing your priorities—relies on your using an effective planning process. The planning process varies slightly for each person, depending on preferences, but, in general, it involves setting aside time each day, week, and month for deciding how you will spend your time and when you plan to enact each of the goals, tasks, and actions that make up your priority list.

Thirdly, the priority-setting key to work–life balance will only be effective if you are able to manage low-priority creep—that is, to avoid letting less important activities, tasks, and goals to take precedence over those you have defined as most important to you.

Since you cannot "do it all," priorities are critical to work–life balance. The nature of time is finite; as a result, you need to make choices on a continual basis about how you would most like to spend your time—which goals, tasks, and actions will most satisfy you when accomplished. Identifying your priorities, putting them into action, and safeguarding them against the competing priorities of others will help you spend your time in a way that leaves you feeling more satisfied with your overall work–life balance.

Create Boundaries

Another key to cultivating work–life balance is creating boundaries. *Boundaries* are limits that you set for yourself that allow you to meet your needs, maintain your priorities, and protect your values. Boundaries also include limits that you set for others in how they interact with you.

Boundaries safeguard important things in your life, such as your time, your energy, and your relationships. Because boundaries provide a structure for maintaining your priorities, boundaries are critical to greater work–life balance. For example, if you have created boundaries for yourself, you will likely find it easier to make choices that align with your desired work–life balance.

People struggling to put this particular key into practice have absent boundaries, loose boundaries, or some combination of both. *Absent boundaries* refer to situations in which you have not put any limits in place to protect something that is important to you. *Loose boundaries* refer to cases in which you have some desired boundary in mind but this boundary is not currently functioning effectively. For a boundary to become effective (e.g., present and sufficiently "firm"), that boundary needs to be defined in a way that is **S**pecific, **M**easurable, **A**ttainable, **R**ealistic, and **T**ime-based.

As discussed earlier in the book, it is often most effective to start with firm boundaries as you experiment with your new boundaries. If you need to, you can always loosen your boundaries later if that feels more comfortable to you.

In sum, boundaries support you in protecting your priorities and enacting the vision you have created for your ideal work–life balance.

Manage Your Day Efficiently

When you use this key—managing your day efficiently—you learn how to spend your time, energy, and attention on the things that are more important to you and you become skilled at using your time, energy, and attention in the most effective, least wasteful way.

People who struggle to use this key face the barrier of leaks in time, attention, and energy. *Leaks* are defined as actions or lack-of-actions that increase demands on a person's time, energy, and/or focus and shift the person away from his or her priorities. Common leaks include multitasking, lack of planning, no support structure, no delegation, clutter and messy office or work space, and social networking black hole.

To manage your day more efficiently, there are specific actions in which you can engage to stop your leaks: these actions are called *plugs*. For example, a plug for multitasking is to set aside time for specific functions in which you just work on a single function at a time: email time, returning phone call time, project time, research time, and so on—whichever functions are relevant to you.

As you begin to use your plugs, it can be helpful to discuss them with those with whom you interact so they are aware of the changes you are making and will understand your new way of operating. You can also seek others' assistance in supporting your new behavior. Ideally, using the plug will create a win–win situation for everyone involved. You will be more efficient and productive and you will be role-modeling behavior that can enhance others' efficiency and productivity.

Design Reasonable Expectations

This key to work–life balance involves …

- eliminating unreasonable expectations and
- creating reasonable expectations.

An *expectation* refers to something that is desired for the future or is anticipated as happening in the future. We have expectations of ourselves, and others have expectations of us as well.

The challenge with expectations occurs when expectations become unreasonable. This typically occurs when you (or others) use words like "must," "should," or "always" or when you (or others) set unmanageable time frames to accomplish certain tasks. Unreasonable expectations typically expand your workload and often challenge your other important priorities, without any guarantee of achieving your desired result.

To move closer toward your ideal work–life balance, you may need to develop more reasonable expectations of yourself and to communicate and negotiate with others to create shared, reasonable expectations. Changing expectations is not an easy process. For many, it is both a difficult and scary endeavor. So, know that this is a significant change—and be gentle on yourself in the process.

Reprioritize Your Values

A *value* can be described as a belief that is extremely important to you, a quality that makes you who you are, or a principle that you uphold in how you choose to live your life. Examples of values include ingenuity, humor, service, directness, vitality, and harmony.

Having a clear idea of what your values are and which ones are most important to you—which are your core values—can be a very useful key to moving toward your desired work–life balance. When you discover that one of your values is incompatible with your other values or with your desired work–life balance, you can make a deliberate choice to continue honoring that value or, instead, to give it a lesser priority and honor a different value that brings you closer to your ideal work–life balance. The first option is referred to as *choosing the status quo*; the second option is referred to as *reprioritizing your values*.

Reprioritizing your values involves shifting your emphasis from one core value onto another. With this approach, you place greater emphasis on a previously unemphasized core value and lesser emphasis on a currently dominant core value. When you reprioritize your values, your behavior changes as a result. For example, if you decide to put more emphasis on your core value of imagination and less emphasis on your core value of perfection, you might decide to take a beginning oil painting class instead of ignoring the course brochure as you have done in the past—because you are less concerned about creating perfect art than you used to be and more focused on giving yourself an outlet for expressing your imagination.

It is common to wait to deal with incompatible values until you are forced to do so—through external challenges or major life crises. Yet, there is no reason to wait for illness or personal crisis before resolving incompatible values. Instead of allowing life circumstances to steer your values, you can take a thoughtful, planned approach to reprioritizing your core values—and move closer to your desired work–life balance in the process.

Navigate an Unbalanced Organizational Culture

Another key that can be helpful on the journey toward work–life balance is learning how to navigate an unbalanced organizational culture. An *unbalanced organizational culture* is one in which the structures, policies, expectations, and/or history of the organization do not support creating an environment in which work–life balance is a concern, a priority, or a possibility. With this key, the term *organization* also refers to your family, as well as any organizations in which you volunteer time, such as religious institutions, professional associations, volunteer organizations, and community associations.

If you want to improve your work–life balance and have identified that one or more of the organizations with which you associate has an unbalanced culture (i.e., is making work–life balance difficult for you), you will need to take action in some capacity if you would like to move closer to your desired work–life balance and stay within the organization.

The action in which you ultimately engage to navigate organizational challenges to work–life balance can take a variety of forms. You might decide to …

- leave the organization and find a new one
- conduct an experiment to change the organizational culture
- rewrite the rules to create a new organizational culture
- set an ultimatum and be comfortable with possible consequences.

In some cases, you might decide to accept the status quo of an unbalanced organization; if this is the approach that you take, ideally, you will be doing so from a deliberate place. When accepting the status quo, I recommend that you schedule a check-in for yourself (e.g., every six months would be a reasonable time frame) and be sure to re-evaluate things at a future date.

Lastly, in the process of creating a solution-oriented plan to deal with an unbalanced organizational culture, consider how the changes you are suggesting will add value to the organization and plan to highlight these as you ask for change. By highlighting the value that your requested changes are likely to bring to the organization, you will have a useful technique for getting other members of the organization invested in supporting your requested change.

Engage in Self-Care

The 7th key to work–life balance is engaging in self-care. Individuals who get stuck on the path to work–life balance sometimes do so because they are missing this particular key—they do not make time to take care of themselves. In these cases, lack of self-care becomes a barrier to work–life balance. In contrast, taking time to care for yourself is likely to enhance your sense of satisfaction with your work–life mix as well as to help you be at your best both at work and in your life in general.

Self-care refers to making choices and taking action in order to increase your physical, mental, emotional, spiritual, and/or social well-being. Self-care involves engaging in activities that help you to rejuvenate, refresh, reinvigorate, and relax. The choices involved with self-care are completely subjective and based on what you desire for yourself: what constitutes self-care is different for each of us.

The reality is that, in order to operate at full efficiency, you need to invest time in yourself. Although leaving self-care out of your day in the short-term may help you temporarily meet deadlines or increase productivity, lack of self-care over the long-term often has negative effects on a person.

Self-care is possible, when the following four points are addressed:

- you commit time and energy to the process
- you learn how to put yourself first at times
- you develop clarity on what is most meaningful and energizing to you
- you create an environment of support.

When these four criteria are present, self-care is likely to be accomplished.

Ultimately, when you nurture yourself, you feel better and usually have a more positive outlook on your life. This pattern then continues—in which feeling better about your life leads to continued self-care and a sense of satisfaction with your work–life balance.

Where Are You Now?

Now that you have reviewed the different keys to work–life balance, let's look at where you are on your journey toward work–life balance, with the goal of appreciating how far you have come toward cultivating your desired work–life balance. It is time to see your progress!

To get a better sense of where you currently are on your journey toward work–life balance, you are about to complete the same *Identifying Your Current Work–Life Balance Satisfaction* fieldwork exercise that you answered in the first chapter (*A Road Map for the Journey*) of the book. The rationale for this particular exercise is to identify your satisfaction level regarding your current work–life balance mix by selecting a number between 1 and 10. As you did earlier, you will also select three words or less to describe your satisfaction level in words.

For example, you might write …

Work–Life Balance Satisfaction Level	Descriptor of How I Feel About My Current Work–Life Balance Situation
8	excited about the future
6	more time/possibilities
9	living life on my terms

When you are ready to assess your current work–life balance satisfaction, continue on to the fieldwork that follows.

 Taking Stock: Take some time now to reflect on your current situation. What is your work–life balance satisfaction now? As you contemplate the answer consider your awareness of the 7 keys and the 7 barriers to using these keys, the choices you have made to eliminate these barriers and put these keys into practice, and new patterns you have developed from doing the fieldwork. As you did earlier in the book, select a number between 1 and 10 to represent your current work–life balance satisfaction level. In addition, write down a new three-word (or less) descriptor of how you feel about your current work–life balance.

Please fill in the blanks shown here (or turn to your *7 Keys Workbook and Journal* or other dedicated work space and conduct the exercise there).

Today's Date: _____

Your Current Work–Life Balance Satisfaction Level (number between 1 and 10): _____

How do you feel about this level (in three words or less):

_____

After you have selected a number and written your descriptor, turn back to the answer you wrote for this exercise the first time you conducted it, when you started reading this book (see the *Identify Your Current Work–Life Balance Satisfaction* fieldwork in the *Road Map for the Journey* chapter, in your *7 Keys Workbook and Journal*, or in your other dedicated work space.) Compare your answers from then with your answers now. What is different between now and when you first started reading the book? Note your differences in feelings, behaviors, energy, awareness, and overall satisfaction. You have invested significant time and energy reading this book—becoming more aware of your choices and behavior—and have likely made significant changes. Take time to pay attention to the results and celebrate even the smallest of improvement in your satisfaction. Tell a friend, go out to lunch or dinner to celebrate, spend an hour at your favorite coffee shop, buy yourself a plant or some new music—choose something that makes you feel special and that helps you honor your hard work. The progress you have made is worth acknowledging and appreciating!

Other questions to consider as you reflect on your current work–life satisfaction include the following:

- Which keys are you making progress on in terms of putting them into practice?

- Which keys and barriers continue to challenge you? Which keys are you having a difficult time putting into practice?

- Which barrier(s) are not an issue for you? Which barriers have you addressed to the level you wished to do with the fieldwork, and which barriers have not been a problem for you from the beginning?

Spend some time reviewing your progress and perspective regarding each key and accompanying barrier in order to evaluate how you wish to continue working toward your more desired work–life balance.

◆ ◆ ◆

You have begun to influence your work–life balance by putting aside time to learn about the 7 keys and 7 barriers, to observe your behaviors, to learn new ways to perceive and operate, and to implement more supportive behaviors. In the process, you may also have begun to transform your life.

Continuing on Your Journey

As mentioned in the book's *Introduction*, the journey toward work–life balance is a continual process. Like the tightrope walker who is always adjusting the pole she is carrying, those of us on a journey toward our ideal work–life balance are also continually making adjustments in our lives to bring about more work–life satisfaction.

As you engaged in the fieldwork for each chapter, you were engaging in the regular hard work needed to cultivate work–life balance. Hopefully, in the process, you have discovered how powerful this kind of effort can be in transforming your life—and your satisfaction with it. In fact, if you were able to do a few, some, or all of the fieldwork exercises in the previous chapters, you are likely at a very different place from when you picked up the book.

If you have not done any fieldwork yet because you wanted on your first reading of the book to get a big picture of the 7 keys before you did anything, I encourage you to revisit the fieldwork exercises in each chapter now or in the near future. By doing so, you will move from "knowing" about the 7 keys to actively working toward putting these keys into practice in your work and life.

The fieldwork exercises will help you develop manageable steps for putting a given key into practice. The exercises will also walk you through a step-by-step approach for trying out the new behavior of using the given key. Changing the way you have always operated can be difficult. A process to follow can make it easier.

For those of you who have completed all of the fieldwork exercises and have a copy of the *7 Keys Workbook and Journal*, you might find it useful to reflect on the *Going Deeper* questions provided there. These questions offer an opportunity to further examine the impact of greater awareness, behavior change, challenges encountered, and new perspectives offered by the chapters and fieldwork exercises covering the 7 keys. If possible, I recommend that you revisit these questions on a regular basis because your responses to them are likely to evolve as you spend more time putting a particular key into practice.

In addition, if you haven't already done so, you may want to create your own "7 Keys Journal" on your computer or in a notebook. You can also pick up a copy of the official *7 Keys Workbook and Journal* (available at *www.7KeysToWorkLifeBalance.com*), which I created to give readers ample space for doing the fieldwork exercises in this book. This workbook also contains extra space for writing about your ongoing journey of developing work–life balance. Using this journal or creating your own will give you a method to regularly check-in with yourself regarding your work–life balance preferences, choices, and actions. It will also help you keep all of your "work" in one place that you can refer back to easily whenever you need to do so.

Lastly, remember, you always have the tools and skills covered in each chapter at your disposal. You can go back and reread chapters and even do fieldwork exercises multiple times. In fact, you will get the most out of the book if you engage in the fieldwork exercises relevant to you on an ongoing basis. As you may recall, the fieldwork invites you to take on one manageable task at a time, such that fieldwork can typically be repeated again and again—to work your way through each of the issues relevant to you and that particular key to work–life balance as your situation changes over a lifetime.

A New Way of Life

You now have a fully loaded tool kit to support you on your journey toward your more desired work–life balance. To make sure you continue in the right direction, schedule regular times to check-in on your progress and make any needed adjustments if you veer too far off your desired course.

Take a moment now to decide whether you will check-in with yourself on a monthly, quarterly, or semi-annual basis. Write down your answer in your *7 Keys Workbook and Journal* or other dedicated work space. Then, add an appointment to your calendar for your next check-in date. Taking just a small amount of time out of your month, quarter, or year will keep your work–life balance preferences a priority.

When it is time to check-in, you can use the fieldwork exercise that follows to conduct the check-in. It parallels the *Taking Stock* fieldwork exercise included earlier in this chapter as well as the *Identifying Your Current Work–Life Balance Satisfaction* fieldwork exercise in the first chapter of the book (*A Road Map for the Journey* chapter). It is provided in the following text as a blank template for you to use in the future.

Check-in/Check-up—A New Way of Life: This exercise, which parallels the previous *Describe Your Preferred Work–Life Balance* Situation (*Road Map for the Journey* chapter) and *Taking Stock* fieldwork (earlier in this chapter), will help you evaluate your current work–life balance satisfaction level at a scheduled time in the future and assess how it compares to the desired feeling/state/experience you want to be moving toward at that future time. (You can download a free template of this exercise at www.7KeysToWorkLifeBalance/ CheckInCheckUp.com.)

To begin, rate your current work–life balance satisfaction level using a number from 1 to 10. Next, return to the statement you wrote up at the very beginning of this process to describe your preferred work–life balance (see the *Describe Your Preferred Work–Life Balance* fieldwork exercise in the *A Road Map for the Journey* chapter). Then answer the following questions.

- How am I feeling about my current state?
- What is working well?
- What is not working well?
- What adjustment(s) can I make to get me closer toward my desired work–life balance feeling/state/experience?
- Revisiting which keys chapters will assist me?

Taking just a small amount of time out of your month, quarter, or year will keep your work–life balance preferences a priority.

Ideally, you will post the statement you created to describe your preferred work–life balance somewhere important so you see it each day. Remember, this is the direction you want your "compass" pointing so you can cultivate a more optimal work–life balance. It also represents the "feeling" you want to be moving toward. And, of course, if your definition of your preferred work–life balance has changed since you first wrote the statement, take some time to readjust it to reflect your current views.

If you have made it to this point in the book, you have had quite a journey. Congratulations! As most people struggle with work–life balance, you are not alone on your path. And, by committing time and energy to getting this far, you are no doubt making changes in how you choose to operate and live. Hopefully, you are feeling some benefits of the work you have put into this process so far. I wish you an enjoyable journey, with many scenic overlooks and pleasurable views along the way!

Thank you for joining me on this journey. As you continue to practice using the 7 keys to work–life balance and to overcome the 7 barriers to work–life balance, I would love to hear your progress. Feel free to drop me an e-postcard at *Julie@7KeysToWorkLifeBalance.com.*

As you revisit your mental travelogue or "photo album," remember to keep these learnings in mind as you navigate the rest of your journey.

- Work–life balance is not an end state to be achieved or a final destination to reach. You will take steps forward to and steps back from your path toward preferred work–life balance.
- Identify the work–life barriers that impact you. Not every barrier will be relevant to you. Some will give you significant challenges and others you will manage quite effectively.
- Know the impact of the barrier on your work and your life. You need to define the cost of a current situation in order to choose to change it.
- Once you choose to make a change, define small steps to take to enact that change. Enjoy your positive results and then take more small steps.
- As your life changes, how the 7 keys and accompanying barriers relate to your life will change, too. Revisit the 7 keys regularly, especially when you feel you are moving away from your desired work–life balance.
- Get assistance along the way. You do not have to go-it-alone. Partners can make the trip more enjoyable and help in avoiding hazards.
- Celebrate along your way. Enjoy where you have been and look forward to where you are going! Bon Voyage!

Appendix

List of Resources for Learning More

Key 1 – Develop Priorities

- *Creative Visualization: Use the Power of Your Imagination to Create What You Want in Your Life* by Shakti Gawain
- *7 Habits for Highly Effective People* by Stephen Covey

Key 2 – Create Boundaries

- *The Assertiveness Handbook* by Randy Paterson
- *My Answer Is No ... If That's Okay With You: How Women Can Say No and (Still) Feel Good About It* by Nanette Gartrell
- *Married to the Job: Why We Live to Work and What We Can Do About It* by Ilene Philipson
- Families and Work Institute: http://www.familiesandwork.org

Key 3 – Manage Your Day Efficiently

- *Getting Things Done* by David Allen
- *Eat That Frog!* by Brian Tracy
- *Organizing From the Inside Out* by Julie Morgenstern
- For tips on Managing email: http://www.eganemailsolutions.com
- To find a professional organizer: http://www.napo.net/get_organized

Key 4 – Design Reasonable Expectations

- *Crucial Conversations* by Kerry Pattterson, et al.
- *Managing Expectations* by Naomi Karten

Key 5 – Reprioritize Your Values

- *Authentic Happiness* by Martin Seligman
- *Now, Discover Your Strengths* by Marcus Buckingham
- *Flow* by Mihaly Csikszentmihalyi
- Values in Action/Signature Strengths Survey: http://www.viastrengths.org

Key 6 – Navigate an Unbalanced Organizational Culture

- *The Five Dysfunctions of a Team: A Leadership Fable* by Peter Lencioni

- *TRUE PROFESSIONALISM: The Courage to Care About Your People, Your Clients and Your Career* by David Maister
- *Good Business: Leadership, Flow and the Making of Meaning* by Mihaly Csikszentmihalyi

Key 7 – Engage in Self-Care

- *The Art of Extreme Self-Care: Transform Your Life One Month at a Time* by Cheryl Richardson
- *Self-Nurture: Learning to Care for Yourself as Effectively as You Care for Everyone Else* by Alice Domar
- *The Harvard Medical School Guide to Men's Health* by Harvey Simon, MD
- *You Staying Young* by Mehmet Oz, MD, and Michael Roizen, MD

Other

- To find a professional coach to assist you on your journey, visit the International Coach Federation: http://www.coachfederation.com
- To find out more about the 7 Keys and get involved in the 7 Keys community, visit http://www.7KeysToWorkLife Balance.com
- For more information about the author, visit http://www.JulieCohenCoaching.com

About the Author

In ten years as a career and leadership coach, Julie Cohen, PCC, has worked with hundreds of clients to clarify and achieve their professional and personal goals. Whether they wanted a promotion, better communication skills, more meaning and satisfaction from their work, or improved leadership capabilities, just about all clients wanted to enhance work–life balance. This led Julie to develop "Overcoming the 7 Barriers to Work–Life Balance"—a program that gives participants tools to identify, clarify, and rectify the challenges that they may be facing.

Julie brings twenty years of experience in corporate, non-profit, and entrepreneurial entities to her work as a coach. Formerly an internal Executive Coach at Cap Gemini Ernst & Young, LLC, she was part of the design team responsible for developing and implementing a national coaching program. She is currently coaching Wharton School MBA Candidates as part of a Leadership Development Program along with a wide array of individual and organizational clients around the world.

Julie has a Bachelor of Arts in Economics from the University of Pennsylvania and a Master of Science in Counseling from Villanova University. She is a graduate of Corporate Coach University International's and Coach University's Training Programs, is a past President of the Philadelphia Area Coaches Alliance, and a member of the International Coach Federation (ICF). Julie has earned the Professional Certified Coach (PCC) designation from the ICF.

Julie's passion and personal focus on work–life balance evolves as she integrates her roles as business owner, mother, wife, pianist, yoga student, and recycling enthusiast.

For more information or to get in touch with Julie about her coaching services, workshops, and public speaking, visit:

www.7KeysToWorkLifeBalance.com

and

www.JulieCohenCoaching.com.